Keto Living Cookbook

Lose Weight with 101 Delicious and Low Carb Ketogenic Recipes

TABLE OF CONTENTS

TO START THE DAY

SOUPS

FISH

MEAT AND POULTRY

SALADS, SIDES AND VEGGIES

FOREWORD

My name is Ella, and all my life I have loved cooking and **really** loved eating. By the time I was 32 years old, I was more than 100 pounds overweight. I weighed more than my three children put together! I was depressed, unmotivated and hungry! All of the time!

That was almost two years ago. Enter my life saver, the Ketogenic Diet.

As you may have learned, our body uses what we eat to give us energy; carbohydrates raise our blood sugar and we produce insulin to get rid of it.

With the help of the insulin, glucose is converted to fat, and stored in our cells.

Goodbye self-esteem. Hello, cellulite!

On the Keto diet, we limit our carbs to fewer than 20-50 grams per day, eat moderate amounts of protein and a good amount of fat for fuel. This keeps us in a state of Ketosis, which is the state in which our body burns fat to give us a good, steady stream energy.

I love to cook and experiment in the kitchen, which is partly responsible for how I got to be so heavy in the first place!

Since the change in diet, I've changed things up, and cooked hundreds of magnificent Keto creations!

The Keto Living Cookbook contains 101 of my very favorite Ketogenic diet recipes, with easy-to-follow instructions for all types of scrumptious meals and snacks prepared right in your kitchen and delivered straight to the table.

What to fix for dinner? There's plenty of variety for everyone.

Need to pack your lunch for the office or job-site? No problem!

Lose Weight with 101 Delicious and Low Carb Ketogenic Recipes

And for that naughty craving? Be prepared by having delicious Keto friendly snacks ready and waiting for you when hunger hits.

This book will become your trusted friend and constant kitchen companion with nutritional info and net carbohydrate count per serving listed for every single recipe.

That's information you want, and need, right at your fingertips.

It's so much easier to reach your goals with the right tools!

Since being on the Keto diet, I've lost the weight and have never felt better. I've turned my life around with equal parts education, encouragement, determination, and a plan in the kitchen.

I just know you're going to love Keto Living in your kitchen and I'm so happy to finally be able to share this selection of recipes with you on your journey towards a healthier new you!

Keto for life!

Ella

DISCLAIMER

Before we get started, a quick note on the nutritional information found at the bottom of each recipe.

Simply put, I've done my best to fastidiously calculate the macro nutrient breakdown, however obviously there will be variations in everyone's exact kitchen creation, due mainly to brand choices, different cuts of meats etc.

So please, understand that as a general rule they should be fairly close in the calculations, and are included primarily to serve as a beneficial guide to keeping you on track.

And as an FYI, the net carb count has been calculated by deducting the dietary fiber from the total carbohydrates.

I certainly hope that the info proves useful and accurate to you, and of course if you wish to double check my calculations on any recipe, I would always recommend that you please do so if you feel the need.

New to this latest reprint, due to popular demand, the ingredients for all recipes are now listed in **both** US Standard **and** Metric. I've also done this for temperatures and measurements where applicable. Enjoy!

Oh, and lastly the standard disclaimer that needs to be added in regards to the Keto diet itself... I recommend anyone undertaking any kind of dietary change to first seek medical advice from your health care provider, or physician.

Also recipes within may not all be suitable for everybody, as each person's condition, needs, allergies, prescriptions etc. are different and myself (the author), publisher and associated parties accept no liability arising from the consumption of any of any recipes created from this book.

Now that's out of the way, let's cook!

A NOTE ON SUGAR SUBSTITUTES

The second book in this series, 'Keto Living 2: Lose Weight with 101 Yummy & Low Carb Ketogenic Savory and Sweet Snacks', includes an informative section on types of sugar substitutes.

This was of course necessary due to the large amount of scrumptious sweet snack recipes that lay within!

For those who don't own Keto Living 2 yet, let me give you a concise version here of what you could do when you encounter recipes that call for sugar substitutes in this book.

In cases where a recipe calls for a **granulated or powdered sugar substitute**, we are looking to use a product that is for all intents and purposes a cup for cup exchange of product by volume, using a granular blend for granular, and powdered for powdered.

In all nutritional panels this has been calculated and added to the totals as if the increasingly popular sweet polyol (or sugar alcohol), Erythritol was used, and this has been calculated at 0.2 carb calories per gram.

Erythritol, when used in direct replacement for sugar is 70% as sweet as sugar and a very nice low carb, low GI ingredient to use that is also dental friendly with minimal complaints of stomach upset at consumption levels of under 50g of product per day.

If the 70% sweetness doesn't quite meet the grade, a couple more tablespoons (per cup) can make it up without altering the structure of most recipes, or better still, blending in a couple of drops of a liquid sweetener of your choice such as Stevia or Sucralose can add a nice synergy to the flavor.

You'll want to avoid granular sugar substitutes that include Maltodextrin or Dextrose as a filler, as the GI and caloric content is actually very similar to sugar. Also avoid falling for packaging claims of zero calories that may not be telling the whole story.

Now, in the case a recipe calls for a **liquid sugar substitute**, I have kept things simple, and simply recommended liquid Stevia.

With liquid Stevia, sweetness intensity can vary from brand to brand depending on the actual percentage of steviol content added to the product (purer is better).

Without getting too techinical, there is also variety in taste and bitterness of Stevia depending on whether the steviol extracted from the plant is Stevioside or the less bitter, and 50% sweeter Rebaudioside A (which I prefer), and this isn't always marked clearly on the label.

Also, if you choose something else like Sucralose as your preferred liquid sweetener, you'll need to adjust the quantity used, as the sweetness of Sucralose is about double that of Stevia.

Aside from the above, feel free to experiment with the many options out there as different substitutes yield different results in the final product, in more ways than one.

There is more information to be found in Keto Living 2 on this subject, but for now, this will help you enjoy creating the recipes contained within this book.

And remember, when it comes to sweetness, if in doubt, a taste test is usually the best practice!

TO START THE DAY

MINI BREAKFAST MUFFINS

A delicious recipe for an instant on the go breakfast!

Makes 6

INGREDIENTS:

½ cup (120g) heavy cream

2 medium eggs

2 ounces (57g) Cheddar cheese, grated

Pinch each black pepper and salt

2 slices back bacon, cooked and crumbled

DIRECTIONS:

1. Pre-heat the oven to 350°F (177°C). Prepare a 6 cup muffin tin with paper cups.

2. In a bowl beat the eggs with the cream and seasonings.

3. Pour the egg mixture into the muffin cups; filling them just under half full.

4. Divide the crumbled bacon among the muffin cups and sprinkle with half of the grated cheese.

5. Bake for 15 – 20 minutes on the center rack of the oven until lightly browned.

6. Remove from the oven and sprinkle with the rest of the cheese.

7. Place under a grill for a moment to melt and brown the cheese.

8. Remove from the heat and eat while still warm.

9. Cool and freeze if there are any left!

10. Reheat in a microwave.

Nutritional Facts per muffin: Calories 109, Fat 8.9g, Carbohydrate 0.7g, Dietary Fiber 0g, Net Carbs 0.7g, Protein 6.4g

SCOTCH EGGS

Great for mornings when you need a breakfast on-the-go! Make these the night before, if you like, as they are just as good cold as they are hot!

Makes 6

INGREDIENTS:

6 large fresh farm eggs

20 ounces (567g) pork sausages, 100% meat

12 slices back bacon, rind removed

6 cocktail sticks

DIRECTIONS:

1. Hard boil the eggs.

2. Cool and peel. Dry thoroughly.

3. Remove the sausage meat from the skins and divide into 6 equal portions.

4. Form each piece into a circle large enough to wrap around the eggs.

5. Carefully wrap each egg making sure that there are no parts of the eggs left uncovered.

6. Place in the fridge for about an hour to 'set'.

7. Pre-heat the oven to 425°F (218°C).

8. Wrap 2 pieces of bacon around each egg and secure with a cocktail stick. Place on a baking tray.

9. Bake for 20 – 25 minutes until cooked and the bacon crisp.

10. Remove from the tray and drain any excess fat.

11. Serve.

Nutritional Facts per Scotch egg: Calories 480, Fat 35.8g, Carbohydrate 1.0g, Dietary Fiber 0g, Net Carbs 1.0g, Protein 36.2g

CHEESY CHORIZO BAKE

Excellent for a weekend treat when you have a little more time to prepare something special. This would also make as excellent lunch dish.

Serves 10

INGREDIENTS:

1 pound (454g) chorizo sausage, ground

4 ounces (113g) onion, chopped

5 ounces (142g) green bell pepper, thinly sliced

12 ounces (340g) spinach, thick stems removed

12 tbsp. heavy cream

1 dozen large eggs

¼ tsp. garlic powder

¼ tsp. onion powder

¼ tsp. salt

¼ tsp. black pepper

8 ounces (227g) Cheddar cheese, grated

8 ounces (227g) ripe cherry tomatoes

DIRECTIONS:

1. Pre-heat the oven to 350°F (177°C).

2. Grease a large casserole dish.

3. Wash the spinach well and place in a saucepan. Cook until tender.

4. Drain the spinach well and mash.

5. In a large skillet, brown the chorizo and set aside in a large bowl.

6. Cook the onion and green pepper in the chorizo fat and add to the sausage.

7. Add the spinach.

8. Beat together the eggs, cream and seasonings to form a thick custard.

9. Add to the sausage and vegetables together with the cheese.

10. Pour the combined mixture into the casserole dish and place in the hot oven.

11. Bake for about 1 hour until brown.

12. Serve warm with the cherry tomatoes on the side for garnish.

Nutritional Facts per portion: Calories 404, Fat 32.5g, Carbohydrate 5.3g, Dietary Fiber 1.6g, Net Carbs 3.7g, Protein 22.9g

HASHED CHILI BACON AND EGGS

The aroma of onions, peppers and bacon in the morning is a true pleasure which gets your taste buds ready for this tangy treat.

Serves 4

INGREDIENTS:

5 ounces (142g) red bell pepper, chopped

3 ounces (85g) chopped onion

1 Jalapenos, sliced with seeds removed

12 slices back bacon

8 large eggs

Oil for frying

DIRECTIONS:

1. Fry the onion, pepper and chili in a skillet until tender but not brown.

2. Chop the bacon finely in a processor or by hand.

3. Add to the vegetable mixture and fry until the bacon is crisp.

4. Fry the eggs.

5. Divide the bacon mixture among 4 plates and top each portion with 2 fried eggs.

Nutritional Facts per serving: Calories 310, Fat 17.5g, Carbohydrate 6.3g, Dietary Fiber 1.2g, Net Carbs 5.1g, Protein 30.8g

MUSHROOM SCRAMBLE

A special cheesy scrambled egg recipe that is full of mushrooms!

Serves 4

INGREDIENTS:

6 ounces (170g) mushrooms

2 tbsp. heavy cream

4 tbsp. butter

1 clove garlic, finely chopped

2 tsp. parsley, chopped

8 large fresh farm eggs

Salt and freshly ground black pepper to taste

1 ounce (28g) Parmesan cheese, shaved

DIRECTIONS:

1. Wipe and chop the mushrooms and sauté until tender in half of the butter in a large skillet.

2. Remove the mushrooms from the skillet and set aside.

3. Crack the eggs into a large jug and beat together until well blended.

4. Add the cream and the seasoning and beat for another minute or so.

5. Melt the remaining butter in the skillet and scramble the egg mixture over a low to medium heat until set but still creamy.

6. Add the mushrooms, garlic and parsley.

7. Cook for a minute longer. Sprinkle with the cheese and serve.

Nutritional Facts per portion: Calories 304, Fat 25.9g, Carbohydrate 2.9g, Dietary Fiber 0g, Net Carbs 2.9g, Protein 16.5g

CHEESE BAKED EGGPLANT

Another recipe for a lazy Sunday morning! Share with your family and friends.

Serves 6

INGREDIENTS:

2 eggplants, each about 12 ounces (340g) before preparation

12 ounces (340g) Romano or mozzarella cheese, grated

4½ ounces (128g) almond flour

4½ ounces (128g) Parmesan cheese, grated

¾ tsp. garlic powder

¾ tsp. Italian herb seasoning

Salt and freshly ground black pepper to taste

3 large fresh eggs

Cooking spray or olive oil

DIRECTIONS:

1. Pre-heat the broiler to its highest heat.

2. Cover a baking sheet with foil. Spray with cooking spray or oil lightly.

3. Beat the egg in a small bowl.

4. Mix together the almond flour, Parmesan cheese, garlic powder, herb seasoning, salt and pepper in a flat dish.

5. Trim the eggplant and cut into 18 slices.

6. Dip each eggplant slice into the egg and then the flour mixture.

7. Place the slices on the baking sheet. Spray each with cooking spray or drizzle on some oil.

8. Broil until golden brown on both sides, turning when appropriate.

9. Watch carefully so the slices do not burn.

10. Pre-heat the oven to 350°F (177°C).

11. Prepare an 8" x 8" baking pan by oiling or spraying as necessary.

12. When the eggplant is brown place a layer in the bottom of the baking pan.

13. Sprinkle over one third of the grated cheese.

14. Repeat with a second layer and cheese and another, third layer ending with cheese on top.

15. Bake for about 25 minutes until bubbly and golden brown.

16. Remove from the oven, cut into squares and serve.

Nutritional Facts per portion: Calories 493, Fat 34.3g, Carbohydrate 16.2g, Dietary Fiber 8.5g, Net Carbs 7.7g, Protein 30.5g

SAUSAGE AND EGG CASSEROLE

A hearty and appetizing breakfast dish, filling and extra cheesy!

Serves 8

INGREDIENTS:

8 large fresh eggs, beaten

1 medium head of cauliflower, chopped

16 ounces (454g) pork sausage, cooked and finely chopped

2 cups (473ml) heavy cream

1 cup (132g) mature Cheddar cheese

1 tsp. salt

1 tsp. English mustard powder

Butter for greasing

DIRECTIONS:

1. Pre-heat the oven to 350°F (177°C).

2. Grease a 9 x 13 casserole dish with butter.

3. In a large bowl mix all of the ingredients until well blended.

4. Pour into the prepared casserole.

5. Bake for 45 – 50 minutes until firm.

6. Serve cut into wedges with some more cheese sprinkled on the top if you fancy.

Nutritional Facts per portion: Calories 439, Fat 37.5g, Carbohydrate 3.3g, Dietary Fiber 0.9g, Net Carbs 2.4g, Protein 22.2g.

BREAKFAST EGG PIZZA

Pizza for breakfast! Well, yes, but the egg way!

Serves 4

INGREDIENTS:

4 large fresh farm eggs

4 slices back bacon

2 ounces (57g) Cheddar cheese, grated

10 slices pepperoni

Salt and freshly ground black pepper

PREPARATION:

1. Pre-heat the oven to 450°F (232°C).

2. In an ovenproof skillet, cook the bacon until crispy. Set aside.

3. Crack the eggs into the bacon fat in the skillet, placing them close together.

4. Sprinkle with salt and pepper.

5. Place the skillet with the eggs into the oven and bake for 5-6 minutes.

6. Remove the skillet from the oven and top the eggs with the Cheddar cheese and pepperoni.

7. Return the skillet to the oven for the cheese to melt and the pepperoni to crisp.

8. When the eggs are completely cooked, top the pizza with bacon.

9. Cut into four and serve whilst still hot.

Nutritional Facts per portion: Calories 241, Fat 17.7g, Carbohydrate 1.1g, Dietary Fiber 0g, Net Carbs 1.1g, Protein 18.8g.

KETO BREAKFAST OMELETTE

This omelette is fit for a king and packed full of flavor to feed a hungry horde!

Makes 2 large omelettes (Serves 4)

INGREDIENTS:

6 large fresh eggs, beaten

4 ounces (113g) bacon, cooked and chopped

4 ounces (113g) ham, chopped

2 ounces (57g) green onion, finely chopped

1 chopped chili pepper

3 ounces (85g) tomatoes, chopped

2 ounces (57g) butter

2 ounces (57g) cheese

Salt and pepper to taste

DIRECTIONS:

1. Mix together the eggs and the seasonings.
2. Pre-heat a large omelette pan, add the butter and pour in the egg mixture.
3. Make an omelette, top with all of the other ingredients.
4. Turn the omelette in half to enclose all of the filling and cut in half.
5. Serve each half on a plate and enjoy!

Nutritional Facts per portion: Calories 474, Fat 38g, Carbohydrate 4.2g, Dietary Fiber 1.0g, Net Carbs 3.2g, Protein 28.8g.

MOZARELLA WAFFLES

You will need a waffle maker for this recipe but it is so delicious you will be glad you bought it!

Makes 12 waffles

INGREDIENTS:

2 cups (290g) cauliflower crumbs, made in a processor

2 cups (226g) mozzarella cheese, shredded

3 ounces (85g) Parmesan cheese, finely grated

4 large fresh eggs

2 tsp. garlic powder

2 tsp. onion powder

1 tsp. pepper

1 tbsp. chives, chopped

½ cup (58g) pumpkin seeds

½ cup (54g) slivered almonds

DIRECTIONS:

1. Pre-heat the waffle maker until the correct temperature is reached.

2. Mix all of the ingredients together in a large jug.

3. Pour ¼ cup egg mixture onto the hot waffle maker.

4. Cook for about 5 minutes. Check to see if it is done. If sticking leave a little longer.

5. Serve each waffle as it is cooked.

Nutritional Facts per portion: Calories 165, Fat 11.6g, Carbohydrate 4.6g, Dietary Fiber 1.2g, Net Carbs 3.4g, Protein 12.0g.

BREAKFAST SMOKED SALMON

This breakfast dish is packed with protein from the egg scramble to irresistible salmon strips. If you love salmon, you will enjoy this!

Serves 2

INGREDIENTS:

4 medium eggs, beaten

½ tsp. dried mixed herbs

1 tbsp. margarine or butter, melted

2 tbsp. milk or cream

Ground black pepper

4 ounces (113g) smoked salmon strips

DIRECTIONS:

1. In a bowl, mix the milk, eggs, herbs and butter. Season to taste.

2. Add to a medium saucepan heated over medium heat and scramble the eggs.

3. Arrange the strips of the smoked salmon on a plate on top of the scrambled eggs. Add a dash of freshly ground pepper.

4. Serve warm and enjoy!

Nutritional Facts per portion: Calories 287, Fat 20.8g, Carbohydrate 1.6g, Dietary Fiber 0g, Net Carbs 1.6g, Protein 24.7g.

MEXICAN OMELETTE À LA KETO

Hola huevos! Usted es muy delicioso con carne! (It's true, these taste great).

Serves 4

INGREDIENTS:

8 eggs

4 ounces (113g) spicy ground beef, cooked

4 ounces (113g) Cheddar cheese, shredded

4 tbsp. salsa

½ avocado, sliced

4 tbsp. sour cream

2 tbsp. black olives, sliced

1 jalapeno pickled pepper, sliced

¼ cup chopped (4g) cilantro

DIRECTIONS:

1. In a bowl, beat the eggs and pour them into a large pre-heated non-stick skillet.

2. Leave the egg to set and form an omelette.

3. Sprinkle over the beef, cheese and salsa.

4. Fold the omelette over and cut into 4 large pieces.

5. Place each piece on a serving plate and top each with a quarter of the avocado and 1 tbsp. sour cream.

6. Sprinkle each serving with olives, pepper and cilantro.

Nutritional Facts per portion: Calories 377, Fat 27.8g, Carbohydrate 3.0g, Dietary Fiber 2.1g, Net Carbs 0.9g, Protein 27.9g.

CREAMY CHOCOLATE SHAKE

A liquid breakfast for those of you on the go!

Makes 2 glasses

INGREDIENTS:

1 scoop chocolate low carb. protein powder

½ cup (120g) light cream

1 tsp. cocoa powder, unsweetened

1 tbsp. sesame oil

1 tsp. psyllium husk

5 drops liquid stevia extract (adjust to taste)

1¼ cups (296ml) water

DIRECTIONS:

1. In a large jug mix the protein powder, cocoa, husk and water and whisk together well.

2. Add the oil and sweetener and whisk again.

3. Add the cream and stir in gently.

4. Drink within half an hour of making the shake.

Nutritional Facts per portion: Calories 219, Fat 16.9g, Carbohydrate 7.0g, Dietary Fiber 5.0g, Net Carbs 2.0g, Protein 13.3g.

SOUPS

CHEESY BROCCOLI SOUP

Warm yourself from the inside out with this healthy and distinctive soup.

Serves 6

INGREDIENTS:

3 tbsp. olive oil

½ cup onion (71g), very finely chopped

¾ cup celery (76g), very finely chopped

Pepper and salt

Cayenne pepper

2 ¾ cups (250g) broccoli florets, well washed to remove any grit

4 pints (1.9L) water

1 cup (239g) heavy cream

2 cups (216g) Gruyere cheese, grated

Creole seasoning to taste (optional)

DIRECTIONS:

1. Put the olive oil to heat in a large saucepan over a medium heat.

2. When hot add the celery and onions and gently sauté for about 5 minutes until softened.

3. Add some salt and a sprinkling of cayenne pepper as the vegetables cook.

4. When the onions are soft add the broccoli florets and sauté for another 5 minutes.

5. Add the water, and salt and pepper to taste.

6. Bring to the boil over a medium heat, stirring constantly.

7. Reduce the heat to a slow simmer and add the cream.

8. Simmer for about 10 minutes, making sure that the soup does not boil again and the cream curdle.

9. Remove the soup from the heat and blend until smooth.

10. Add ¾ of the grated cheese to the soup and stir well until it has melted.

11. Check the seasoning and serve in individual bowls.

12. Sprinkle the remaining cheese on top and season with Creole seasoning if liked.

Nutritional Facts per portion: Calories 298, Fat 26.2g, Carbohydrate 4.7g, Dietary Fiber 1.5g, Net Carbs 3.2g, Protein 12.5g.

CABBAGE AND CHICKEN SOUP

Get your spoon ready to dive into this amazing combination of cabbage and chicken in a garlicky broth.

Serves 4

INGREDIENTS:

2 cups (482g) organic chicken broth

4 ounces (113g) fresh green cabbage, finely shredded

1 ounce onion (28g), grated

1 clove garlic, minced

3¾ ounces (106g) chicken breast, poached and diced

2 ounces (57g) butter

2 ounces (57g) olive oil

2 ounces (57g) heavy cream

Salt and pepper to taste

DIRECTIONS:

1. In a large sauce pan, sauté the cabbage, garlic and onions in the olive oil and butter.

2. When the vegetables are soft add the broth and the chicken.

3. Cover and simmer over a low heat for about 10 minutes until the vegetables are very soft.

4. Add some water if the soup becomes too thick at this stage.

5. Remove from the heat and stir in the cream.

6. Pureed if desired.

7. Season to taste and serve.

Nutritional Facts per portion: Calories 338, Fat 31.6g, Carbohydrate 3.4g, Dietary Fiber 0.9g, Net Carbs 2.5g, Protein 11.8g.

BEEF AND VEGETABLE SOUP

Try this classic vegetable soup that tastes just like Mom used to make! If there is any left over, it freezes well for a second serving.

Serves 8

INGREDIENTS:

3 pounds (1.35kg) beef

1½ pints (710ml) beef broth

1 x 8 ounce (227g) can tomato sauce

3 ounces (85g) onion, diced

4 ounces (113g), celery finely chopped

14 ounces (397g) green cabbage, shredded

3 ounces (85g) fresh green beans, chopped

1 clove garlic, crushed

1 tbsp. salt

Pinch pepper

¼ tsp. cayenne pepper

1 bay leaf

4 tbsp. olive oil

DIRECTIONS:

1. Finely chop the beef and brown on all sides in the oil in a large sauce pan.

2. Add the vegetables and sauté for a couple of minutes.

3. Add all of the other ingredients and bring to the boil.

4. Turn down to a simmer and leave bubbling slowly for a couple of hours until the meat is tender.

5. Serve hot!

Nutritional Facts per portion: Calories 421, Fat 18.1g, Carbohydrate 7.2g, Dietary Fiber 2.5g, Net Carbs 4.7g, Protein 54.9g.

CREAMY CHICKEN SOUP

A mouth-watering creamy goodness of cauliflower, c

Serves 6

INGREDIENTS:

4 cups (948ml) well flavored chicken broth

½ cup (71g) onion, finely chopped

1 clove garlic, minced

2 large celery stalks, finely chopped

3 ounces (85g) carrot, finely grated

1 tsp. black pepper

½ tsp. powdered paprika

2 tsp. xanthan gum

2 tsp. chicken stock powder

12 ounces (340g) small cauliflower florets

2 tbsp. butter

2 cups (478g) heavy cream

2 cups (280g) cooked chicken, diced

½ cup (30g) fresh parsley, chopped

Salt to taste

DIRECTIONS:

1. In a large sauce pan melt the butter.

2. Sauté the onion, garlic, celery and carrot until translucent and tender.

3. Sprinkle over the black pepper, 2 tsp. parsley, paprika, xanthin gum and stock powder.

4. Add the cauliflower and the broth to the sauce pan.

5. Bring to the boil.

6. Once boiling, reduce the heat to a simmer and cover the sauce pan with a lid.

7. Simmer for about 25 minutes until all of the vegetables are tender, stirring from time to time.

8. Remove from the heat and stir in the cream, cooked chicken and the rest of the parsley.

9. Replace on the heat and warm through carefully. Do not let the soup boil.

10. Adjust the seasoning and add salt as required.

11. Serve.

Nutritional Facts per portion: Calories 282, Fat 20.6g, Carbohydrate 8.5g, Dietary Fiber 2.6g, Net Carbs 5.9g, Protein 16.9g.

TANGY CHICKEN AND PEPPER SOUP

Make a double quantity of this heart-warming soup as it freezes beautifully and is just as good the second time around.

Serves 6

INGREDIENTS:

1½ cups (213g) onions, chopped

5 ounces (142g) leek, washed and chopped

3 cloves garlic, crushed

1 cup (124g) zucchini, finely chopped

1 cup (124g) red bell pepper, chopped

1 x 15 ounce (425g) can chopped tomatoes

8 ounces (227g) tomato sauce

1 tsp. chicken stock powder

1 tsp. vegetable stock powder

Salt and pepper to taste

½ tsp. each cayenne and chili pepper (or to taste)

11 cups (2607ml) water

3 tbsp. butter

1½ pounds (681g) chicken thigh, chopped

8 ounces (227g) cream cheese

1 tbsp. sour cream and 3 tbsp. grated Cheddar cheese to garnish

DIRECTIONS:

1. Add the butter to a large sauce pan and melt over a medium heat.

2. Add the onion, leek, garlic, pepper and zucchini.

3. Stir fry until soft but not brown.

4. Add the chopped tomatoes and the tomato sauce and stir well.

5. Add the water, stock powders and spices.

6. Reduce the heat to a simmer and simmer the soup for about an hour.

7. Meanwhile fry off the chicken meat in a pan until cooked through.

8. Add to the soup after simmering and cook together for another 10 minutes.

9. Add the cream cheese and adjust the seasoning.

10. Serve in individual bowls while still hot and top with a little sour cream and grated cheese.

Nutritional Facts per portion: Calories 475, Fat 29.3g, Carbohydrate 14.0g, Dietary Fiber 3.0g, Net Carbs 11.0g, Protein 39.0g.

MUSHROOM SOUP WITH FENNEL AND LEEKS

Mushrooms, fennel and leeks combine well in this creamy soup.

Serves 8

INGREDIENTS:

16 ounces (454g) cremini mushrooms, sliced

2 cups (174g) fennel bulb, sliced

2 cups (178g) leeks, sliced

2 pints (946ml) heavy cream

4 cups (948ml) rich, flavorful chicken stock (unsalted)

8 tbsp. unsalted butter

½ tsp. salt

6 ounces (170g) dry sherry

DIRECTIONS:

1. In a large saucepan melt the butter and add the mushrooms. Fry gently until lightly browned.

2. Add the fennel and the leeks and cook the vegetables together until soft.

3. Remove from the pan. Add the sherry and scrape off all of the vegetable pieces remaining at the bottom of the saucepan.

4. Set over a high heat and allow the alcohol in the sherry to burn off. Add the cream and simmer together gently to reduce by about half.

5. Add the stock and the vegetables and heat through until piping hot.

6. Puree the soup before serving in individual bowls.

Nutritional Facts per portion: Calories 586, Fat 56.1g, Carbohydrate 11.1g, Dietary Fiber 1.4g, Net Carbs 9.7g, Protein 6.6g.

FRESH SUMMER SOUP

A hot or cold soup high in vitamins and minerals with the tang of sour cream!

Serves 4

INGREDIENTS:

2 pints (946ml) beef broth

4 ounces (113g) fresh parsley

4 ounces (113g) sorrel leaves

3½ ounces (99g) sour cream

1 large egg, yolk only

¼ cup (59ml) olive oil

DIRECTIONS:

1. Wash the parsley and the sorrel under plenty of cold water, drain.

2. Cut the sorrel into long strips and roughly chop the parsley.

3. Put the broth into a large saucepan and bring to a boil over a medium heat.

4. Add the sorrel and parsley and simmer together for a few minutes. Remove from the heat and set aside.

5. Strain about 1½ cups of liquid off the soup and place in a small pan. Allow to cool.

6. Mix the egg yolk with the sour cream in a small bowl. Beat in the oil.

7. Add this to the separated soup liquid by whisking it in carefully. You do not want the egg to cook.

8. Add this creamy mixture back into the main soup pot and serve immediately.

9. If cooled do not reheat.

Lose Weight with 101 Delicious and Low Carb Ketogenic Recipes

Nutritional Facts per portion: Calories 266, Fat 25.4g, Carbohydrate 2.8g, Dietary Fiber 0.9g, Net Carbs 1.9g, Protein 7.8g.

MUSHROOM AND CRAB SOUP

A delicately flavored soup with a hint of white wine!

Serves 6

INGREDIENTS:

1 pound (454g) fresh mushrooms, wiped and sliced

¼ cup (35g) onion, finely chopped

4 tbsp. butter

4 cups (948ml) well flavored chicken broth

¼ cup (59ml) dry white wine

8 ounces (227g) crab meat

½ cup (120g) heavy cream

2 tbsp. parsley, finely chopped

Salt and freshly ground black pepper to taste

DIRECTIONS:

1. Melt the butter in a large saucepan and sauté the onion and the mushrooms until soft.

2. Remove some of the mushrooms to add to the soup at the end of the cooking.

3. Add the chicken broth and the white wine to the onions and mushrooms.

4. Puree the mixture until smooth and then simmer for a few minutes to allow for the flavors to blend.

5. Stir in the crab meat, the reserved mushrooms, cream and parsley.

6. Season to taste and serve in individual bowls.

Nutritional Facts per portion: Calories 170, Fat 12.6g, Carbohydrate 4.9g, Dietary Fiber 0.9g, Net Carbs 4.0g, Protein 8.2g.

SUMMER AVOCADO SOUP

Soup on a warm summer's evening to entertain or just to spoil yourself!

Serves 8

INGREDIENTS:

3 cups (717g) heavy cream

3 cups (711ml) avocado puree

2 Jalapeno peppers, seeded and chopped

½ cup (8g) cilantro, finely chopped

2 tsp. powdered cumin

1 tsp. salt

DIRECTIONS:

1. Place all of the ingredients into a food processor.

2. Whizz until well blended and smooth.

3. Chill in the refrigerator until you are ready to serve.

4. Stir gently, if necessary, before placing in soup bowls to serve.

5. Garnish with extra cilantro if liked.

Nutritional Facts per portion: Calories 327, Fat 32.8g, Carbohydrate 8.8g, Dietary Fiber 3.9g, Net Carbs 4.9g, Protein 2.6g.

CHILLED CREAMY CELERY SOUP

This lovely soup should be made with fresh ingredients to bring out its full flavor. It is packed with zucchini, cucumber and celery that blend well together.

Serves 4

INGREDIENTS:

20 ounces (567g) zucchini, unpeeled

15 ounces (425g) cucumber, unpeeled

1 medium red bell pepper

5 celery stalks

1 cup (239) heavy cream

2 tbsp. fresh dill, chopped

4 tbsp. extra virgin olive oil

Salt and pepper to taste

DIRECTIONS:

1. Thoroughly wash all of the vegetables and cut into small dice.

2. Place the vegetables in a processor or juicer.

3. Add the fresh cream and olive oil.

4. Process or juice until well blended.

5. Test for seasoning and add salt and pepper if necessary.

6. Serve immediately in chilled bowls, garnish with dill.

Nutritional Facts per portion: Calories 279, Fat 25.7g, Carbohydrate 12.8g, Dietary Fiber 3.3g, Net Carbs 9.5g, Protein 3.8g.

FISH

CRISPY BAKED FISH

Tasty baked fish with a very crunchy outside – yum!

Serves 6

INGREDIENTS:

2 pounds (908g) firm white fish fillets – 6 fillets

2 tbsp. oil

4 tbsp. mayonnaise

1 cup (70g) pork rinds, crushed

Salt and pepper

DIRECTIONS:

1. Pre-heat the oven to 450°F (232°C).

2. Line a large baking sheet with foil and drizzle some olive oil onto it.

3. Mix the crumbed pork rinds with the seasonings and place on a large plate.

4. Coat the fish on both sides with mayonnaise and dip them individually into the seasoned crumbs.

5. Place apart on the prepared baking tray.

6. Bake for 15 – 20 minutes until brown and crispy. Do not overcook.

Nutritional Facts per portion: Calories 392, Fat 22.5g, Carbohydrate 2.3g, Dietary Fiber 0g, Net Carbs 2.3g, Protein 43.2g.

HERBY SALMON WITH LEMON

A delicious way to prepare fresh salmon – buttery and oozing flavor!

Serves 6

INGREDIENTS:

6 tbsp. butter, at room temperature

1 ounce (28g) parsley, chopped

3 cloves garlic, finely chopped

6 salmon fillets – about 1½ pounds (681g)

6 slices lemon

Salt and pepper

DIRECTIONS:

1. Pre-heat the oven to 375°F (191°C).

2. Cut 6 pieces of foil large enough to wrap around each piece of fish.

3. Mix together the butter, garlic and parsley in a small bowl.

4. Place a salmon fillet in the centre of each piece of foil and season with salt and pepper.

5. Make a few cuts in each salmon fillet with a sharp knife and rub the butter evenly among the pieces.

6. Place the lemon slices on top of the fish.

7. Wrap up the 'parcels' and seal the foil at the edges.

8. Place on a baking tray and bake for 12 – 15 minutes in the hot oven.

9. Open the packets to serve piping hot.

Nutritional Facts per portion: Calories 258, Fat 18.6g, Carbohydrate 1.5g, Dietary Fiber 0g, Net Carbs 1.5g, Protein 22.4g.

TUNA AND SHRIMP CAKES

These delicate fish cakes are ideal to serve for lunch or a light dinner and would go well with a green salad.

Serves 4

INGREDIENTS:

6 ounces (170g) tuna meat, tinned

6 ounces (170g) fresh shrimp, cleaned and cooked

2 tbsp. green bell pepper, finely chopped

1 tbsp. green onion, finely chopped

2 tbsp. celery stalk, finely chopped

1 clove garlic, finely chopped

1 tbsp. butter

1 large egg

¼ tsp. paprika

Pinch cayenne pepper

1 ounce (28g) Cheddar cheese, grated

¼ cup (18g) pork rinds, crushed

Olive oil for frying

DIRECTIONS:

1. Mince about half of the shrimp and finely chop the rest.

2. In a skillet, sauté the celery, bell pepper, green onion and garlic in the butter until tender.

3. Combine the tuna meat, shrimp and vegetables in a bowl and mix in the egg.

4. Stir in all of the seasoning, cheese and the pork rinds.

5. Mix to a stiff paste and refrigerate for about an hour until firm.

6. Heat some olive oil in a skillet; make sure that there is enough to cover the bottom of the pan.

7. Form the fish cakes into 8 small equal portions and flatten slightly.

8. Place in the hot oil and fry, turning gently to ensure that they are brown on both sides.

9. Serve hot.

Nutritional Facts per portion: Calories 215, Fat 11.3g, Carbohydrate 1.7g, Dietary Fiber 0g, Net Carbs 1.7g, Protein 27.7g.

SUMMER CRAB CAKES

Enjoy these on a sunny summer's day! They are served with a tangy mayo dressing too.

Serves 6

INGREDIENTS:

1 pound (454g) crab meat, shredded

¼ cup (59ml) olive oil

¼ cup (28g) flax seed flour

3 tbsp. coconut flour

1 tsp. salt

1 tsp. mustard powder

1 tsp. garlic powder

Pinch freshly ground black pepper

2 small celery stalks, finely chopped

½ red bell pepper, finely chopped

4 small green onion, minced

2 large fresh eggs

1½ tbsp. Worcestershire sauce

Butter for frying

8 tbsp. mayonnaise

Chili sauce to taste

DIRECTIONS:

1. In a large bowl mix together all of the ingredients (except for the mayonnaise, chili sauce and butter), to make a firm dough.

2. With damp hands form the mixture into 12 small patties and flatten to about ½ inch (1.25cm) thick.

3. Heat some butter in skillet and fry the crab cakes in batches until brown and cooked through. About 5 minutes each side.

4. Serve hot with a tangy mayonnaise made from 8 tablespoons mayonnaise mixed with enough chili sauce to your taste.

Nutritional Facts per portion: Calories 372, Fat 31.0g, Carbohydrate 7.4g, Dietary Fiber 3.1g, Net Carbs 4.3g, Protein 13.5g.

FISH PIE WITH A CHEESY CRUST

A creamy, tasty pie! So good that you won't miss the pastry or the potato topping!

Serves 4

INGREDIENTS:

1 pound (454g) firm white fish

1 cup (239g) heavy cream

1¼ pounds (568g) cauliflower

7 ounces (198g) Cheddar cheese, grated

2 ounces (57g) butter

1 large carrot, sliced

2 ounces (57g) spinach, washed

1 tsp. dill

1 tsp. parsley

1 fish broth cube

1 tsp. pepper

½ cup (119ml) boiling water

Pinch of salt

Olive oil to cook

Butter

DIRECTIONS:

1. Heat some oil in a skillet and fry the fish fillets until cooked.

2. Cool and flake removing any bones and skin. Set aside.

3. Steam the cauliflower and carrot until soft.

4. While the vegetables are steaming, place the flaked fish in a large sauce pan together with the cream, spinach and herbs which have been finely chopped.

5. Add the broth cube which has been dissolved in the boiling water and the pepper.

6. Cook over a low heat until the spinach has wilted – do not boil.

7. When the vegetables are cooked, remove them from the steamer.

8. Set the cauliflower aside and dice the carrots.

9. Mix the carrots into the fish mixture.

10. Blend the cauliflower until smooth and then add half of the cheese and a pinch of salt.

11. Pre-heat the oven to 375°F (191°C).

12. Grease a casserole dish with some butter.

13. Put the fish pie filling into the dish and top with the cauliflower mash.

14. Bake in the oven for about 40 minutes until the cauliflower starts to crisp.

15. Sprinkle with the rest of the cheese and broil until the cheese is bubbly and golden brown.

16. Serve hot.

Nutritional Facts per portion: Calories 553, Fat 48.3g, Carbohydrate 13.1g, Dietary Fiber 4.5g, Net Carbs 8.6g, Protein 16.6g.

FISH SUPREME

Use any flat fish for this recipe which has a tang from the sour cream and lemon juice. A simple dish to prepare when dinner needs to be on the table!

Serves 4

INGREDIENTS:

1½ pounds (681g) of flat fish of your choice, cut into 4 pieces

½ cup (57g) cheese, Cheddar is best

¼ cup (25g) Parmesan cheese, finely grated

½ cup (119ml) sour cream

½ cup (120g) mayonnaise

2 tsp. lemon juice

3 green onions, finely chopped

1 tsp. cayenne pepper

DIRECTIONS:

1. Pre-heat the oven to 425°F (218°C).

2. Lightly grease a baking dish.

3. In a medium bowl mix the cheeses, mayo, cream, onion, cayenne and lemon juice.

4. Arrange the fish in the baking dish and cover with the cheese mixture.

5. Put in the oven and bake for 10 – 12 minutes.

6. Reduce the heat to 350°F (177°C) and continue cooking for 15 more minutes until the fish flakes easily.

7. Serve hot with a salad of your choice.

Nutritional Facts per portion: Calories 478, Fat 25.3g, Carbohydrate 9.9g, Dietary Fiber 0g, Net Carbs 9.9g, Protein 51.3g.

STUFFED SOLE WITH SHRIMP

A delicious recipe for sole which with the addition of white wine is raised to a level nothing short of delectable!

Serves 4

INGREDIENTS:

1½ pounds (681g) of sole filets

6 green onions, finely chopped

¼ cup (59ml) lemon juice, freshly squeezed

6 cloves garlic, finely chopped

½ pound (227g) cream cheese

1 pound (454g) cooked shrimp

1 cup (237ml) dry white wine

Salt and pepper to taste

2 tbsp. paprika

6 tbsp. butter

1 cup (239g) heavy cream

DIRECTIONS:

1. Pre-heat the oven to 375°F (191°C).

2. Lightly grease a baking dish.

3. In a small bowl mix the lemon, garlic, onion and half of the wine. Set aside.

4. Spread a layer of cream cheese on each sole filet and sprinkle with salt, pepper and paprika.

5. Arrange the fish in the baking dish and cover with the cooked shrimp. Drizzle with the lemon mixture.

6. Cover the baking dish with foil and bake in the oven for 20 – 25 minutes.

7. Meanwhile, melt the butter in a small pan.

8. Stir in the cream and the rest of the wine. Bring to the boil.

9. Reduce the heat and simmer until the mixture is reduced by half.

10. When the fish has finished cooking remove it from the pan onto a serving plate.

11. Pour the cream mixture into the baking dish and with a spoon mix it in with the fish juices.

12. Taste and season as necessary. Pour over the fish on the serving plate.

Nutritional Facts per portion: Calories 756, Fat 50.7g, Carbohydrate 11.1g, Dietary Fiber 2.0g, Net Carbs 9.1g, Protein 53.4g.

MEAT AND POULTRY

MIDDLE EASTERN CHICKEN

Chicken with a lemony tomato flavor.

Serves 4

INGREDIENTS:

1½ pounds (681g) chicken breast fillets

6 tbsp. olive oil

8 cloves garlic

Freshly squeezed lemon juice, about 2 juicy lemons

1 tbsp. heavy cream

4 tbsp. tomato sauce

1 pound (454g) green beans

DIRECTIONS:

1. Finely chop the garlic and dice the chicken into bite sized pieces.

2. In a small bowl mix together the oil, lemon juice, garlic and the tomato sauce.

3. Place the chicken into a bowl and pour the oil mixture over it, rubbing it into the pieces of chicken with your hands.

4. Cover the bowl with plastic wrap and put it into the fridge to marinate for about an hour – you could leave it overnight if you wished.

5. When you are ready to cook, place a skillet on the stove over a high heat. When hot add the chicken and marinade.

6. Brown off over the high heat and then turn the heat down and let the chicken cook for another 20 minutes or so, stirring occasionally.

7. While the chicken is cooking, prepare and cook the green beans as you like them.

8.   Just before serving add the cream to the chicken and stir in well.

9.   Leave to simmer for a few more minutes.

10.   Serve hot with the green beans.

Nutritional Facts per portion: Calories 564, Fat 35.2g, Carbohydrate 11.0g, Dietary Fiber 4.2g, Net Carbs 6.8g, Protein 51.9g.

SPICY CHICKEN KEBABS

This one is a real crowd pleaser! Share and enjoy!

Serves 4

INGREDIENTS:

12 ounces (340g) chicken breasts

2 red bell peppers

2 yellow bell peppers

Powdered paprika

2 tbsp. olive oil

2 lemons

Salt and pepper

8 ounces (227g) haloumi

DIRECTIONS:

1. Soak some wooden kebab skewers in water.

2. Pre-heat the oven to 400°F (204°C).

3. Chop the chicken breasts into cubes of about 1 inch (2.5cm).

4. Seed and chop the peppers into squares.

5. Thread the chicken pieces and the pepper alternately onto the skewers.

6. Place the completed skewers onto an oven tray and drizzle with olive oil.

7. Sprinkle with lemon juice, paprika and olive oil.

8. Place the kebabs in the oven for about 20 minutes until cooked.

9. Meanwhile, slice the haloumi and place it into skillet.

10. Cook over a high heat for about 5 minutes, turning it frequently until it is nicely browned.

11. Place the cooked skewers on a serving plate, together with the haloumi and serve.

12. Add any other vegetables you wish but remember to add them into your carb. Count!

Nutritional Facts per portion: Calories 421, Fat 25.0g, Carbohydrate 7.2g, Dietary Fiber 2.5g, Net Carbs 4.8g, Protein 39.0g.

CREAMY HERB CHICKEN

Piquant chicken, bursting with tarragon flavor and white wine!

Serves 4

INGREDIENTS:

6 tbsp. butter

2 small onions, thinly sliced

2 cloves garlic, finely chopped

½ cup (119ml) chicken broth

½ cup (119ml) dry white wine

½ cup (120g) heavy cream

8 ounces (227g) cream cheese (full cream)

1 tsp. dried tarragon

1 tsp. French herb seasoning

1 tsp. chicken spice

4 uncooked chicken breasts

DIRECTIONS:

1. Preheat the oven to 350°F (177°C).

2. Grease an oven proof dish using a little of the butter.

3. Place a skillet over a medium heat and add 2 tbsp. butter.

4. Sauté the onions, garlic and tarragon in the butter until soft.

5. Remove and set aside.

6. Add 2 more tbsp. butter to the skillet and over a low heat, add the wine and cheese.

7. Stir until well mixed and then add the cream, herb seasoning and spice.

8. Pour the chicken broth into the dish and add the chicken breast.

9. Spoon over the onion mixture followed by the cheesy cream.

10. Bake for about 50 minutes until cooked through and bubbly.

11. Serve.

Nutritional Facts per portion: Calories 781, Fat 55.8g, Carbohydrate 6.6g, Dietary Fiber 0.7g, Net Carbs 5.9g, Protein 56.5g.

EXTRA QUICK CHEESY CHICKEN

A superbly quick tomato and chili chicken dish to prepare for your family and friends!

Serves 8

INGREDIENTS:

4 tbsp. butter

2 medium onions, finely chopped

4 cloves garlic, minced

8 large chicken breast fillets

2 x 12 ounce (340g) cans chopped tomatoes with chili

8 ounces (227g) full fat cream cheese, diced

½ cup (119ml) whipping cream

½ cup (119ml) chicken broth

½ tsp. cayenne pepper

2 tsp. dried cumin

Salt to taste

Grated Cheddar cheese to garnish

DIRECTIONS:

1. Wash and pat dry chicken breasts, slice thickly.

2. In a non-stick skillet, over medium heat, melt the butter and sauté the onions and garlic until tender.

3. Add the chicken slices, and cook on both sides until the juices run clear.

4. Turn the heat down to low, and add the tomatoes and chili.

5. Cover, and allow chicken to simmer for 10 minutes.

6. Add the spices, cream cheese and cream.

7. Stir until the cheese is melted and chicken and vegetables are coated.

8. Add extra broth to thin the sauce if it is too thick.

9. Season with salt to taste.

10. Serve hot topped with some grated Cheddar cheese.

Nutritional Facts per portion: Calories 561, Fat 32.2g, Carbohydrate 7.6g, Dietary Fiber 1.7g, Net Carbs 5.9g, Protein 58.1g.

NOODLES AND CHICKEN

Tofu noodles add variety to your chicken meals! Add some mouth-watering cheese, spinach and bacon and you have a meal fit for a king!

Serves 4

INGREDIENTS:

1 pound (454g) shirataki noodles

1 large fresh egg

1 cup (132g) Cheddar cheese

½ cup (113g) mascarpone cheese

½ cup (119ml) sour cream

½ tsp. each salt and pepper

1 cup (107g) chopped spinach

8 ounces (227g) chicken breast, cooked and chopped

1 ounce (28g) bacon, cooked and chopped

3 tbsp. Parmesan cheese

Butter for greasing

DIRECTIONS:

1. Pre-heat the oven to 350°F (177°C).

2. Prepare a 3 pint (1.4L) casserole dish by greasing with a little butter.

3. In a large colander rinse the noodles very well in hot water. You will have to do this several times to ensure they smell fresh.

4. Chop up any long noodles into bite sized pieces. Leave small shapes whole.

5. Once rinsed dry the noodles with a paper towel.

6. Using a non-stick pan continue the drying process by tossing the noodles in the dry pan until all the moisture has evaporated.

7. Set the noodles aside.

8. In a large bowl beat the egg and then stir in the cheeses, sour cream and spices until well mixed.

9. Gently mix in the chicken, spinach and bacon.

10. Add the dried noodles and then pour everything into the prepared casserole dish.

11. Sprinkle the top with the Parmesan cheese and bake for about 25 minutes until bubbly.

12. Brown the cheese under the broiler if wished.

Nutritional Facts per portion: Calories 417, Fat 27.2g, Carbohydrate 7.2g, Dietary Fiber 2.8g, Net Carbs 4.4g, Protein 36.4g.

TEX-MEX CHICKEN

Spicy chicken with red and green bell peppers for that southern taste!

Serves 4

INGREDIENTS:

4 tbsp. olive oil

12 ounces (340g) chicken breast, cut into strips

4 tbsp. powdered paprika

2 tbsp. turmeric

Salt and pepper

Garlic powder to taste

1 large onion, thinly sliced

1 cup (124g) green bell pepper, cut into strips

1 cup (124g) red bell pepper, cut into strips

1 cup (260g) tomato salsa

8 ounces (227g) Cheddar cheese, grated

DIRECTIONS:

1. Pre-heat the oven to 425°F (218°C).

2. Prepare a casserole by oiling it lightly.

3. Fry the chicken strips in the oil in a skillet until brown on all sides.

4. Add the spices and seasoning.

5. When the chicken is nearly done remove from the skillet and set aside.

6. Add the onions and peppers to the skillet and cook for a few minutes until tender but still with a bite.

7. Put the chicken into the casserole and top with the pepper mixture.

8. Spoon the salsa on top and sprinkle over the grated cheese.

9. Place in the oven for about 10 minutes to heat through and for the cheese to melt.

10. Serve hot.

Nutritional Facts per portion: Calories 537, Fat 36.3g, Carbohydrate 10.2g, Dietary Fiber 2.7g, Net Carbs 7.5g, Protein 42.8g.

CHICKEN AND SAUSAGE BAKE

With mushrooms and cream this dish hints of a stroganoff! Serve it with cabbage for a low carb. meal but with noodles for those who can eat them!

Serves 4

INGREDIENTS:

6 ounces (170g) Italian spicy chicken sausage

6 ounces (170g) chicken, cooked and chopped

1 small onion, chopped

6 ounces (170g) mushrooms, sliced

4 ounces (113g) cream cheese

½ cup (120g) heavy cream

½ cup (119ml) water mixed with ½ cup (119ml) dry white wine

Pinch each chili flakes, salt and pepper

1 tsp. olive oil

3 cups (210g) green cabbage, finely shredded

DIRECTIONS:

1. Skin the sausage and crumble the meat. Brown it in a large skillet.

2. Add the onion and mushrooms and sauté for 5 minutes until translucent and tender.

3. Add the chopped chicken and sauté for a couple more minutes.

4. Lower the heat and add the cream, cream cheese, water and wine and spices.

5. Simmer for 6 minutes to allow the flavors to blend. Do not let it boil.

6. Meanwhile cook the cabbage as liked.

7. Serve the cabbage onto plates and top with the creamy chicken.

Nutritional Facts per portion: Calories 359, Fat 22.7g, Carbohydrate 10.8g, Dietary Fiber 2.4g, Net Carbs 8.4g, Protein 22.5g.

CAULIFLOWER AND CHICKEN BAKE

A flavorful combination which is tasty enough to serve to both your family and friends!

Serves 4

INGREDIENTS:

4 cups (496g) cooked cauliflower

3 cups (420g) chicken, grilled and shredded

1 cup (242g) canned tomatoes mixed with chili

8 ounces (227g) Cheddar cheese, grated

1 large green onion, chopped

1 clove garlic

¼ red bell pepper, chopped

1 tbsp. parsley, chopped

1 tbsp. cilantro, chopped

1 tbsp. olive oil

Pinch ground cumin

DIRECTIONS:

1. Pre-heat the oven to 375°F (191°C).

2. Place the green onion, garlic, pepper, parsley, cilantro and oil into a blender and whizz until a thick sauce is formed. Add more oil if liked.

3. In a medium bowl, place the shredded chicken, cooked cauliflower, tomatoes and the sauce from the blender.

4. Mix gently together with the cumin.

5. In a casserole dish place half of the chicken mixture and half of the cheese on top of it.

6. Add a second layer of chicken and cheese.

7. Place in the hot oven and cook through until the cheese has melted and everything is hot – about 20 minutes.

8. Serve.

Nutritional Facts per portion: Calories 455, Fat 25.7g, Carbohydrate 8.7g, Dietary Fiber 3.3g, Net Carbs 5.4g, Protein 47.1g.

LEMONY CHICKEN

A simple tangy tasting chicken dish which may be served with a Greek or Italian salad! Add some camembert or brie cheese for a special occasion.

Serves 6

INGREDIENTS:

1 pound (454g) chicken breast fillets

1 cup (237ml) olive oil

1 lemon, juiced

1 tbsp. fresh rosemary, finely chopped

Salt and pepper

DIRECTIONS:

1. Prepare a marinade for the chicken by mixing together the oil, lemon juice and rosemary. Season with pepper.

2. Chop the chicken into cubes and add to the marinade.

3. Cover and place in the fridge for at least two hours.

4. Remove from the fridge and sprinkle with salt to taste.

5. Heat a non-stick skillet over a medium heat and fry the chicken in it until cooked, the lemon juice has evaporated and the cubes are nicely browned.

6. Drain the chicken and serve hot with some cheese and a fresh, crisp salad.

Nutritional Facts per portion: Calories 292, Fat 22.5g, Carbohydrate 1.3g, Dietary Fiber 0.5g, Net Carbs 0.8g, Protein 22.0g.

HERBED LEG OF LAMB

An aromatic lamb dish that is just right for Sunday lunch.

Serves 6

INGREDIENTS:

3 pound (1.35kg) leg lamb, boned weight

10 cloves garlic, minced

1 tsp. each thyme and rosemary

1 tbsp. lemon juice, freshly squeezed

1 tbsp. olive oil

2 tbsp. butter

½ cup (119ml) red wine, dry

DIRECTIONS:

1. Pre-heat the oven to 450°F (232°C).

2. Trim the leg of lamb and with a sharp knife, slash the fatty side of the meat.

3. Mix the garlic, thyme, rosemary, lemon juice and olive oil together in a small bowl to form a paste.

4. Rub this mixture into the leg well.

5. Tie up the lamb if necessary with twine to make a good shape and place in a roasting pan.

6. Place in the hot oven and roast for 20 minutes at the high temperature.

7. Reduce the heat to 325°F (163°C) and continue to roast the meat for about 50 minutes until the desired stage of doneness.

8. Remove the meat from the oven and cover with foil. Rest for 10 minutes.

9. Add the wine to the pan and deglaze it by scrapping off the

drippings from the meat.

10. Add the butter to the pan and reduce by about half over a medium high heat.

11. Remove the twine from the meat if used, slice and serve with the sauce.

Nutritional Facts per portion: Calories 600, Fat 44.4g, Carbohydrate 2.2g, Dietary Fiber 0g, Net Carbs 2.2g, Protein 40.5g.

LAMB CUTLETS WITH CAULIFLOWER AND BROCCOLI

Broiled lamb cutlets with steamed vegetables for a quickly prepared midweek dinner!

Serves 4

INGREDIENTS:

8 lamb cutlets

2 cups (182g) broccoli florets

2 cups (248g) cauliflower florets

4 tsp. Worcestershire sauce

2 tsp. tarragon vinegar

1 tsp. onion powder

1 tsp. French mustard

½ cup (119ml) water

Salt and freshly ground black pepper

2 tbsp. olive oil

1 tbsp. parsley, chopped

1 tbsp. chives, chopped

2 tsp. slivered almonds, toasted

DIRECTIONS:

1. Cook the broccoli and cauliflower as you wish.

2. Mix together the sauce, vinegar, onion powder, mustard and water.

3. Season to taste.

4. Rub the sauce mixture into the chops and baste with a little olive oil.

5. Broil under a preheated broiler until cooked to your preference.

6. Turn half way through the cooking time; baste with any sauce that may drip into the pan.

7. Serve with the vegetables and garnish with the chopped herbs and the toasted almonds.

Nutritional Facts per portion: Calories 433, Fat 18.8g, Carbohydrate 7.4g, Dietary Fiber 2.6g, Net Carbs 4.8g, Protein 53.4g.

KETO LAMB WITH ROSEMARY

Lamb chops with a creamy mixture of vegetables to tempt your taste buds!

Serves 4

INGREDIENTS:

1 pound (454g) lamb, boned and finely chopped

2 tbsp. butter

4 tbsp. heavy cream

½ cup (119ml) olive oil

4 tbsp. frozen peas

1 medium onion, chopped

½ cup (62g) red bell pepper, chopped

1 medium carrot, grated

1 lamb broth cube

Pinch dried rosemary

Salt and pepper

DIRECTIONS:

1. Heat the oil in a skillet and gently fry together the lamb, bell pepper, onion, crumbled broth cube and rosemary.

2. Cook the carrot and peas until soft in a little water. Drain and add to the lamb mixture.

3. Add the butter and the cream and heat through. Do not boil.

4. Season to taste and serve.

Nutritional Facts per portion: Calories 560, Fat 45.0g, Carbohydrate 6.7g, Dietary Fiber 1.8g, Net Carbs 4.9g, Protein 33.4g.

LAMB WITH A CAJUN TWIST

Piquant spices from the south blend deliciously with these lamb cutlets. Serve with tasty coleslaw for a well-rounded Keto meal.

Serves 4

INGREDIENTS:

8 lamb cutlets

2 tbsp. French Dijon mustard

2 tbsp. thick plain yogurt

1 tbsp. white wine vinegar

1 green bell pepper, finely sliced

5 cups (350g) Savoy cabbage, shredded finely

2 green onions, finely sliced

1 tsp. caraway seeds, toasted

¼ cup (2g) fresh dill

2 tsp. Cajun spice mix

Olive oil

DIRECTIONS:

1. Make the coleslaw by mixing together, in a small bowl, the mustard, yogurt, and vinegar.

2. Place the cabbage, pepper, onions, chopped dill and caraway seeds in a large salad bowl and toss together with the mustard mixture.

3. Refrigerate until serving.

4. Rub the chops with 2 tsp. of olive oil and the Cajun spice.

5. Fry the chops in some oil in a hot skillet until cooked to your liking.

6. Serve with the coleslaw.

Lose Weight with 101 Delicious and Low Carb Ketogenic Recipes

Nutritional Facts per portion: Calories 407, Fat 16.0g, Carbohydrate 10.3g, Dietary Fiber 3.9g, Net Carbs 6.4g, Protein 52.0g.

SPICED LAMB KEBABS

Ground lamb with a spicy flavor which gives the warmth of the Mediterranean!

Serves 4

INGREDIENTS:

1 pound (454g) lamb, ground

1 small onion, finely chopped

4 cloves garlic, minced

1 fresh egg

6 tbsp. coconut oil

½ tsp. each of ground cumin, clove, cinnamon, black pepper, chili powder and nutmeg

1 tbsp. salt

2 tbsp. coconut flour

1 jalapeño pepper, finely chopped and seeded

DIRECTIONS:

1. In a large bowl mix together all of the ingredients, except the coconut oil. Refrigerate overnight,

2. Form the meat into 8 sausage shapes and press onto 4 metal skewers.

3. Melt the coconut oil and brush the meat before placing on a hot grill.

4. Turn often and brush with more oil as needed.

5. 8 – 10 minutes should be sufficient for them to cook and brown. Serve while hot.

Nutritional Facts per portion: Calories 430, Fat 30.2g, Carbohydrate 4.9g, Dietary Fiber 1.8g, Net Carbs 3.1g, Protein 34.1g.

BARBEQUED PORK RIBS

These ribs may be cooked in a crock-pot or in the oven – very versatile.

Serves 8

INGREDIENTS:

4 pounds (1.8kg) meaty pork ribs

6 ounces (170g) tomato sauce

1 cup (237ml) water

4 tbsp. vinegar

8 tbsp. Worcestershire sauce

2 tbsp. dry mustard

2 tbsp. chili powder (or to taste)

8 tbsp. granulated sugar substitute

DIRECTIONS:

1. Pre-heat the oven to 350°F (177°C).

2. Put a large skillet on a high heat and add the ribs in batches, to brown on both sides.

3. If using a crock-pot, oil the sides and base, otherwise have ready a large roasting pan.

4. Add the ribs to the container being used.

5. In a small bowl mix together all of the remaining ingredients and pour evenly over the ribs to coat them well.

6. Cover the crock-pot and cook for 8 – 10 hours. If using the oven, cover with foil and bake for about an hour.

7. When cooked serve hot with plenty of table napkins to mop up the sauce and to wipe fingers!

Nutritional Facts per portion: Calories 663, Fat 41.3g, Carbohydrate 6.9g, Dietary Fiber 1.4g, Net Carbs 5.5g, Protein 61.3g.

THAI GREEN CURRY

Eastern flavors with pork, coconut and lime. A quick dinner tasty enough to serve to your guests!

Serves 4

INGREDIENTS:

1½ ounces (43g) shallot, finely chopped

¼ cup (59ml) olive oil

16 ounces (454g) fresh pork, diced

1 tsp. fresh ginger, grated

2 tsp. Thai green curry paste

14½ ounces (411g) chicken broth

13½ ounces (383g) full cream coconut milk

Salt to taste

2 green onions, sliced diagonally

½ cup (21g) fresh basil, shredded

1 tbsp. freshly squeezed lime juice

DIRECTIONS:

1. Heat the oil in a large skillet or wok over a high heat.

2. Add the shallots and pork and stir fry until brown and nearly cooked.

3. Turn down the heat and add the ginger and curry paste. Stir to make sure the meat is evenly coated.

4. Add the broth, coconut milk and salt to taste.

5. Bring to the boil and reduce by a half, about 15 minutes.

6. Stir in the green onions, basil and lime juice.

7. Serve in individual bowls.

Lose Weight with 101 Delicious and Low Carb Ketogenic Recipes

Nutritional Facts per portion: Calories 555, Fat 42.9g, Carbohydrate 9.8g, Dietary Fiber 3.2g, Net Carbs 6.6g, Protein 34.8g.

SAGE AND GARLIC PORK CHOPS

These chops have a tasty butter sauce which can be used over other grilled meats if you wish to make some changes to your diet.

Serves 4

INGREDIENTS:

2 ounces (57g) butter, melted

1 small onion, chopped

1 tsp. dried sage

3 cloves garlic, finely chopped

½ cup (30g) fresh parsley, chopped

2 tbsp. olive oil

4 thick loin pork chops

Salt and pepper

DIRECTIONS:

1. Heat the oil and butter in a large skillet.

2. Sprinkle the chops with seasoning and brown in the skillet.

3. Set the chops aside, keep warm.

4. In the same skillet fry the onions and garlic until the onion is tender.

5. Add the herbs, stirring well.

6. Place the chops back into the skillet and cover with a lid.

7. Turn the heat to low and simmer for 10 minutes to warm through.

8. Serve with green vegetables.

Nutritional Facts per portion: Calories 419, Fat 35.2g, Carbohydrate 2.9g, Dietary Fiber 0.7g, Net Carbs 2.2g, Protein 23.9g.

CREAMY PORK WITH MAYONNAISE

Creamy pork with rosemary is a marriage made in heaven! Try it and see!

Serves 4

INGREDIENTS:

1 pound (454g) boneless pork steaks, about ½ inch (1.25cm) thick

2 tbsp. fresh rosemary, finely chopped

1 tsp. onion powder

Pinch freshly ground black pepper and cayenne pepper

7 tbsp. mayonnaise

1 small onion, thinly sliced

2 tbsp. olive oil

½ chicken stock cube, dissolved in ¾ cup (178ml) of boiling water

1 tbsp. corn flour dissolved in 1 tablespoon of cold water

2 tbsp. of freshly chopped parsley

DIRECTIONS:

1. Pre-heat the oven to 350°F (177°C).

2. Flatten the pork steaks with a mallet and sprinkle with onion powder, pepper and cayenne.

3. Place the steaks on an oiled baking tray.

4. Spread the mayonnaise over the steaks. Sprinkle with half of the rosemary.

5. Separate the onion rings and spread over the meat. Sprinkle with the remaining rosemary.

6. Mix together the chicken stock and the cornflour and pour around the pork steaks to keep them moist.

7. Bake for about 40 minutes until the pork is cooked.

8. Serve with the gravy from the pan and sprinkle with parsley.

Nutritional Facts per portion: Calories 418, Fat 24.8g, Carbohydrate 10.2g, Dietary Fiber 1.2g, Net Carbs 9.0g, Protein 39.8g.

CRISPY PORK SCHNITZEL

Crispy and tasty with not a bread crumb in sight!

Serves 4

INGREDIENTS:

1½ pounds (681g) boneless pork loin slices

2 tbsp. olive oil

2 tbsp. butter

½ cup (119ml) milk

2 eggs

2 ounces (57g) flax seed, ground

1 ounce (28g) sesame seed, ground

Pinch pepper and salt

DIRECTIONS:

1. Pound each pork slice until really thin.

2. Mix the flaxseed, sesame, salt and pepper and spread out on a large plate.

3. Beat the egg and milk together and season to taste.

4. Coat the pork slices with egg and milk and then put them in the dry mixture. Make sure they are evenly coated.

5. Place on a large plate covered with baking paper and rest in the fridge for 15 minutes.

6. Heat the oil and butter in a large non-stick skillet over a medium high heat.

7. Lay the pork slices in the oil and fry carefully until cooked and golden brown. About 4 minutes for each side.

8. Drain on paper towel and serve whilst still hot.

9. Serve with a crunchy green salad and lemon slices if liked.

Nutritional Facts per portion: Calories 486, Fat 30.3g, Carbohydrate 8.4g, Dietary Fiber 6.3g, Net Carbs 1.9g, Protein 34.7g.

PORK CHOPS WITH A CHEESE CRUST

Flavorful pork chops with a Parmesan cheese coating. Delicious!

Serves 4

INGREDIENTS:

2 pound (908g) boneless pork chops

2 tbsp. olive oil

¼ cup (59ml) French Dijon mustard

½ tsp. thyme, chopped

Pinch pepper

¾ tsp. dried marjoram and basil, mixed

½ tsp. garlic powder

¾ cup (75g) Parmesan cheese, grated

DIRECTIONS:

1. Preheat the oven to 400°F (204°C).

2. Line a baking sheet with parchment paper and set aside.

3. Whisk together the mustard, oil, herbs and spices in a small bowl.

4. Season the chops with pepper and brush them on both sides with the mustard mixture.

5. Press the grated Parmesan into both sides of the chops.

6. Place the chops on the prepared baking sheet and bake for 20 - 25 minutes.

7. The crust should be brown and slightly crispy and the pork should be cooked all the way through.

Nutritional Facts per portion: Calories 492, Fat 21.0g, Carbohydrate 1.4g, Dietary Fiber 0g, Net Carbs 1.4g, Protein 68.5g.

CARAMELIZED ONIONS WITH SPICY SAUSAGE

A favorite of everyone who tries this recipe! The servings are quite generous so make sure you share it!

Serves 8

INGREDIENTS:

1 pound (454g) hot breakfast sausage, skinned

1 medium brown onion, diced

2 tbsp. butter

2½ tbsp. garlic, finely chopped

8 ounces (227g) button mushrooms, sliced

3 tbsp. tomato paste

1 tbsp. chili sauce

9 extra-large fresh eggs

1 cup (113g) mature Cheddar cheese, grated

½ cup (50g) Parmesan cheese, grated

Salt and pepper

DIRECTIONS:

1. Pre-heat the oven to 350°F (177°C).

2. Have ready a large baking dish.

3. Caramelize the onions and garlic in the butter, in a large skillet. Season with salt and pepper. About 25 minutes over a low heat.

4. In another skillet brown the sausage meat.

5. When the sausage is nearly cooked. Add the mushrooms, tomato paste and chili sauce.

6. Crack the eggs into a large bowl and beat well.

7.   Add the cheeses to the beaten eggs.

8.   Place the meat mixture into the baking dish and pour the egg mixture evenly over the top.

9.   With the back of a spoon make indentations into the sausage to form 'puddles' of egg.

10. Place in the oven and bake for 35 – 40 minutes until golden brown.

Nutritional Facts per portion: Calories 404, Fat 31.7g, Carbohydrate 4.9g, Dietary Fiber 0.9g, Net Carbs 4.0g, Protein 24.9g.

HAM AND CHEESE WITH CAULIFLOWER MASH

*If you enjoy the combination of ham and cheese you will enjoy making
and eating this for dinner. Add a leafy green salad on the side.*

Serves 8

INGREDIENTS:

1 large head cauliflower, cut into pieces

14 ounces (397g) ham, diced

8 ounces (227g) cream cheese

½ cup (119ml) sour cream

2 ounces (57g) green onion, chopped

Salt and pepper to taste

8 ounces (227g) sharp Cheddar cheese

Paprika to garnish

DIRECTIONS:

1. Pre-heat the oven to 350°F (177°C).

2. Have ready a greased 3 quart casserole with a lid.

3. Cook the cauliflower until tender and drain very well.

4. Place the cauliflower into the casserole.

5. In a bowl mix together the cream cheese, sour cream, onion,
   seasoning, ham and Cheddar.

6. Add to the cauliflower and sprinkle with paprika.

7. Cover and bake for 35 minutes. Uncover and continue baking
   for another 15 minutes to brown the top.

*Nutritional Facts per portion: Calories 353, Fat 26.7g, Carbohydrate 9.7g,
Dietary Fiber 3.5g, Net Carbs 6.2g, Protein 20.1g.*

SAUSAGE AND BELL PEPPERS

Sausage with an Italian flavor- the children will surely be asking for more!

Serves 4

INGREDIENTS:

1¼ pounds (568g) Italian sausages

2 tbsp. olive oil

1 large green bell pepper, chunked

1 large red pepper, thickly sliced

6 ounce (170g) onion, chopped

2 cloves garlic, finely chopped

¾ cup (178ml) tomato spaghetti sauce

5 ounces (142g) mozzarella cheese, grated

DIRECTIONS:

1. Brown the sausages in a skillet over a medium heat.

2. When the sausages are partially cooked add in the peppers, onion and garlic.

3. Continue to cook until the sausages are done and the vegetables are still crisp.

4. Take the sausages out of the skillet and slice into chunky bite sized pieces. Return to the pan.

5. Stir in the spaghetti sauce and cover.

6. Simmer for 5 – 8 minutes until all is piping hot.

7. Sprinkle with the cheese and serve.

Nutritional Facts per portion: Calories 743, Fat 60.0g, Carbohydrate 18.0g, Dietary Fiber 3.8g, Net Carbs 14.2g, Protein 31.6g.

SMOKY BACON BURGERS

The smoky flavor comes from the bacon and some smoked Mozzarella cheese! Grill over the barbeque for a great outdoor treat!

Serves 8

INGREDIENTS:

2 tbsp. chia seeds, powdered

1¼ cups (296ml) water

2 pounds (908g) ground beef

10 slices bacon, chopped

2 large red onions, finely chopped

6 tbsp. bacon fat, from the bacon as it is cooking

Rock salt

Freshly ground black pepper

1 tsp. mixed Mediterranean dried herbs

12 ounces (340g) smoked mozzarella cheese, sliced into 8

DIRECTIONS:

1. Mix the ground chia seeds with the water and set aside to form a gel.

2. In a large bowl mix well together the meat, seasoning and herbs.

3. Add the chia gel and mix well to ensure that it is evenly distributed.

4. In a skillet, brown the bacon until crisp. Crumble and drain on a paper towel. Add to the beef.

5. Sauté the onion in the bacon fat and add it, along with the fat to the beef.

6. Form the meat mixture into 8 even sized patties and fry in a hot skillet, turning until browned and cooked through.

7. Top each patty with a slice of cheese and place under a broiler to melt.

8. Sprinkle each one with bacon and serve.

Nutritional Facts per portion: Calories 487, Fat 25.6g, Carbohydrate 7.1g, Dietary Fiber 2.2g, Net Carbs 4.9g, Protein 54.4g.

SAUSAGE STIR FRY WITH CRISP CABBAGE

This recipe could not be easier – it is colorful and it tastes superb!

Serves 4

INGREDIENTS:

12 ounces (340g) pure meat pork sausage

4 ounces (113g) onion, sliced

4 cups (356g) green cabbage, coarsely chopped

1 large red bell pepper, chopped

Salt and pepper

2 tbsp. bacon fat

DIRECTIONS:

1. Skin the sausage and fry in a large skillet, breaking the meat up as it cooks.

2. As the sausage is browning add the onion and allow to cook until soft and translucent.

3. Add the bacon fat, bell pepper and seasoning.

4. Sauté for a short while longer.

5. Add the cabbage and stir fry until it just begins to soften but still retains some crispness.

6. Season to taste and serve.

Nutritional Facts per portion: Calories 360, Fat 30.4g, Carbohydrate 9.1g, Dietary Fiber 3.2g, Net Carbs 5.9g, Protein 10.7g.

BEEF STEAK AND MUSHROOMS

This steak is exquisite and it just takes a few moments to make. Use a stronger cheese if you wish and leave the steaks whole for a bigger portion!

Serves 4

INGREDIENTS:

4 x 6 ounce (170g) beef steaks

1 cup onion (142g), sliced

2 green bell peppers, sliced

8 ounces (227g) mushrooms, sliced

¼ cup (59ml) olive oil

Butter to sauté

2 ounce (57g) mild white cheese, sliced

Salt and pepper

DIRECTIONS:

1. Season and broil the steaks as you would like them.

2. Cut into bite sized pieces and place in a heatproof dish.

3. Sauté the onion, mushrooms and pepper in a little butter and the olive oil until caramelized.

4. Season to taste and spoon over the steak.

5. Layer the cheese slices on top and melt under a broiler until brown and bubbly.

Nutritional Facts per portion: Calories 541, Fat 30.2g, Carbohydrate 8.2g, Dietary Fiber 2.4g, Net Carbs 5.8g, Protein 57.8g.

KETO LASAGNA

Now this title is an anomaly – surely not lasagne on a Keto diet? Does the pasta have to be pasta?

Serves 12

INGREDIENTS:

4 large zucchinis, sliced thinly, lengthwise

2 cups (464g) cream cheese

2 eggs

4 ounces (113g) mozzarella cheese, shredded

3 ounces (85g) Parmesan cheese

2 pounds (908g) ground beef

4 cloves garlic, finely chopped

1 x 4 ounce (113g) can tomato paste

1 cup (245g) tomato pasta sauce

Salt, pepper, chili powder to season

Oil for greasing

DIRECTIONS:

1. Grease a 3 quart casserole dish with a little oil.

2. Lay the zucchini slices on a paper towel and sprinkle them with salt.

3. Turn the slices over and sprinkle the other side.

4. Cover with more paper towel to soak up the excess moisture.

5. Press down firmly and leave for about 15 minutes.

6. Meanwhile, pre-heat the oven to 350°F (177°C).

7. Fry the beef with the garlic in a large skillet until brown and cooked through, add seasoning, tomato paste and pasta sauce.

8. Mix well and cook together for a few minutes. Remove from the heat and set aside.

9. Beat the eggs and mix in the cream cheese, seasoning and Parmesan cheese. Blend well.

10. Remove the paper towels from the zucchini when it has drained and wipe off any remaining water.

11. Place a layer of the cream and cheese mixture at the bottom of the casserole dish, top with some meat sauce and then a layer of zucchini.

12. Repeat these layers at least 3 times until you run out of ingredients.

13. Top the lasagne with the shredded mozzarella.

14. Place the dish in the oven and bake for about 45 minutes.

15. Place under a broiler to brown the top some more if you wish.

16. Remove from the heat and let the dish stand for about 15 minutes before serving.

Nutritional Facts per portion: Calories 383, Fat 24.1g, Carbohydrate 8.9g, Dietary Fiber 1.9g, Net Carbs 7.0g, Protein 33.6g.

BEEFY LOAF WITH HERBED VEGETABLES

This ideal for a family lunch or dinner and tastes just like the one Mom used to make!

Serves 6

INGREDIENTS:

1½ pounds (681g) ground beef

6 eggs

1 cup (142g) onion, finely chopped

½ cup (90g) tomato, finely chopped

1 cup (72g) mushrooms, finely chopped

1 cup (124g) red bell pepper, finely chopped

¼ cup (237ml) Worcestershire sauce

2 tbsp. mixed dried herbs

1 tbsp. sweet paprika

Onion salt and pepper to taste

3 tbsp. olive oil

3 tbsp. chopped chives

3 tbsp. chopped parsley

DIRECTIONS:

1. Pre-heat the oven to 375°F (191°C).

2. Mix together the beef, eggs, Worcestershire sauce, herbs and paprika.

3. Sprinkle with onion salt and pepper to taste.

4. Mold into a loaf shape and wrap in foil.

5. Bake in the oven for about 40 minutes or until cooked through.

6. Sauté the tomato, mushrooms, bell pepper and onion in the olive oil and when cooked sprinkle with the chopped parsley and chives.

7. Remove the meat loaf from the oven and leave to rest for 10 minutes.

8. Slice and serve covered with the sautéed vegetables.

Nutritional Facts per portion: Calories 368, Fat 18.8g, Carbohydrate 7.3g, Dietary Fiber 1.8g, Net Carbs 5.5g, Protein 41.1g.

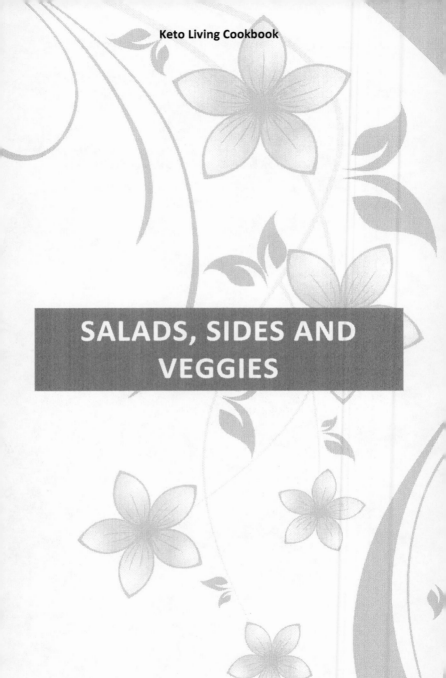

SALADS, SIDES AND VEGGIES

KALE À LA SOFRITO

A flavorful way to serve kale either as a side or as a full meal!

8 servings as a side dish

INGREDIENTS:

4 slices back bacon

½ cup (119ml) olive oil

4 ounces (113g) onion, coarsely chopped

6 cups (780g) kale, after washing, de-stemming and tearing

4 tbsp. sofrito sauce

Salt and pepper to taste

Water for cooking the kale

DIRECTIONS:

1. In a medium sauce pan, add the oil and brown the bacon.

2. Sauté the onions until caramelized and a golden color.

3. Add the kale leaves to the bacon and onion.

4. Add the sofrito sauce and season to taste.

5. Cover the kale with cold water, bring to the boil.

6. Reduce the heat and simmer, for about 25 minutes until tender.

7. Drain off the liquid and serve.

Nutritional Facts per portion: Calories 179, Fat 15.3g, Carbohydrate 7.0g, Dietary Fiber 1.4g, Net Carbs 5.6g, Protein 5.7g.

TANGY TUNA SALAD

Simply toss this together for a tasty and filling salad.

Serves 4

INGREDIENTS:

2 cups (292g) solid canned tuna in oil

8 tbsp. mayonnaise

4 tsp. hot chili sauce

2 large celery stalks

1 tsp. cayenne pepper

3 tsp. dried cilantro

DIRECTIONS:

1. Chop the celery stalks into small pieces.

2. Drain the tuna and place in a large bowl

3. Mix the mayonnaise, cilantro, celery and cayenne pepper together very well.

4. Add the chili sauce.

5. Toss into the tuna and lightly mix everything together. Refrigerate for half an hour.

6. Serve and enjoy.

Nutritional Facts per portion: Calories 285, Fat 17.1g, Carbohydrate 8.0g, Dietary Fiber 0.5g, Net Carbs 7.5g, Protein 24.1g.

BROCCOLI AND MUSHROOMS

A veggie dish just on its own or with chicken perhaps!

Serves 6

INGREDIENTS:

2 pounds (908g) broccoli, cooked and well drained

2 tbsp. butter

¼ cup (59ml) olive oil

6 ounces (170g) mushrooms, chopped

1 small onion, finely chopped

2 celery stalks, finely chopped

¼ cup (59ml) mayonnaise

½ pound (227g) Cheddar cheese, shredded

½ tsp. each salt and pepper

Garlic powder to taste

2 tsp. parsley, chopped

DIRECTIONS:

1. Pre-heat the oven to 350°F (177°C).

2. Grease a 2 quart casserole.

3. Sauté the onion, mushrooms and celery in the butter and oil.

4. Mix together the broccoli, onion mix and all of the other ingredients and place in the prepared casserole.

5. Place in the hot oven and bake for about 30 minutes until lightly brown.

6. Serve.

Nutritional Facts per portion: Calories 360, Fat 28.7g, Carbohydrate 15.1g, Dietary Fiber 4.5g, Net Carbs 10.6g, Protein 14.9g.

MARINATED BABY TOMATOES

A light and tangy salad to accompany cold meats, cheese or fish!

Serves 8

INGREDIENTS:

16 ounces (454g) baby tomatoes, halved

3 green onions, finely chopped

3 tbsp. parsley, chopped

1 tbsp. granulated sugar substitute

1½ tsp. garlic salt

½ tsp. pepper

¾ cup (178ml) light olive oil

½ cup (119ml) red wine vinegar

DIRECTIONS:

1. Place the green onions, tomatoes and parsley in a bowl.

2. Mix together all of the other ingredients. Taste for seasoning.

3. Pour over the tomatoes.

4. Let stand at room temperate for a couple of hours before serving.

Nutritional Facts per portion: Calories 188, Fat 19.3g, Carbohydrate 4.8g, Dietary Fiber 1.1g, Net Carbs 3.7g, Protein 1.1g.

SPINACH SALAD

Serve this fresh salad as it is or you could use it as an accompaniment at a barbeque!

Serves 6

INGREDIENTS:

10 ounces (284g) fresh baby spinach

6 ounces (170g) baby tomatoes, halved

1 small red onion, very thinly sliced

8 ounces (227g) bacon, crisped and crumbled

2 hardboiled eggs, peeled and sliced

½ cup (119ml) ranch dressing

2 avocado pears, mashed

DIRECTIONS:

1. Mix together the avocado and dressing until it is well mixed and smooth.

2. Place all of the other ingredients into a large bowl and toss in the avocado dressing.

3. Serve immediately before the spinach wilts.

Nutritional Facts per portion: Calories 386, Fat 30.8g, Carbohydrate 6.6g, Dietary Fiber 6.2g, Net Carbs 0.4g, Protein 19.3g.

BROCCOLI CRUNCH

Bacon adds the crunch! You could also make this salad with cauliflower or a mixture of cauliflower and broccoli.

Serves 6

INGREDIENTS:

1 pound (454g) fresh broccoli, chopped

8 ounces (227g) bacon

4 ounces (113g) Gouda cheese, shredded

1 cup (237ml) mayonnaise

¼ cup (59ml) olive oil

2 tbsp. white wine vinegar

2 tbsp. granulated sugar substitute

Salt and pepper to taste

DIRECTIONS:

1. Chop up the bacon and fry in its own fat until crispy.

2. Drain in a paper towel.

3. Beat together the mayonnaise, vinegar, olive oil and sugar substitute until well blended.

4. Season to taste.

5. Place the broccoli, bacon and cheese into a bowl and pour over the mayonnaise.

6. Toss together. Leave to chill for an hour before serving.

Nutritional Facts per portion: Calories 524, Fat 42.7g, Carbohydrate 15.6g, Dietary Fiber 2.0g, Net Carbs 13.6g, Protein 21.2g.

SPECIAL EGG SALAD

Crunchy onion and celery lift this egg salad beyond the ordinary!

Serves 6

INGREDIENTS:

8 eggs, hard boiled and peeled

½ cup (119ml) mayonnaise

¼ cup (59ml) olive oil

1 tbsp. white wine vinegar

¾ tsp. salt and pepper, mixed

2 tsp. granulated sugar substitute

1 small red onion, chopped

2 celery stalks, chopped

2 tbsp. parsley, chopped

DIRECTIONS:

1. Mix together all of the ingredients except the eggs in a medium sized bowl.

2. Coarsely chop the eggs and stir them carefully into the mayonnaise mixture.

3. Cover and place in the fridge to chill before serving.

Nutritional Facts per portion: Calories 241, Fat 20.8g, Carbohydrate 7.1g, Dietary Fiber 0g, Net Carbs 7.1g, Protein 7.8g.

KETO RATATOUILLE

Serve hot or cold as a salad, this versatile vegetable dish tastes delicious both ways!

Serves 8

INGREDIENTS:

½ cup (119ml) olive oil

½ cup (71g) onion, chopped

16 ounces (454g) eggplant, cubed

1 large yellow bell pepper

8 ounces (227g) zucchini, chopped

4 cloves garlic, finely chopped

12 ounces (340g) tomatoes, skinned and chopped

¼ cup (59ml) vegetable broth

Few drops chili sauce

½ cup (21g) fresh basil, torn

Salt and pepper to taste

DIRECTIONS:

1. Heat the olive oil in a skillet and fry the onion until it is sizzling.

2. Add the eggplant cubes and cook for about 5 minutes.

3. Sprinkle the onions and eggplant with salt.

4. Add the yellow pepper to the skillet and cook for a couple of minutes. Finely add the zucchini and cook through.

5. Add the garlic at this stage followed by the tomatoes.

6. Stir well before adding the broth.

7. Your dish is ready when the tomatoes collapse and the eggplant is very soft.

8. Season to taste and add the chili sauce.

9. Toss in the torn basil and serve.

Nutritional Facts per portion: Calories 147, Fat 13.0g, Carbohydrate 8.3g, Dietary Fiber 3.4g, Net Carbs 4.9g, Protein 1.8g.

PEPPERED SUMMER SQUASH

Serve hot or cold as a salad, this versatile vegetable dish tastes great both ways!

Serves 8

INGREDIENTS:

1¾ pounds (795g) yellow summer squash

6 green onions, chopped

6 ounce (170g) can green chilis, chopped

3 cloves garlic, finely chopped

1 tbsp. olive oil

½ cup (119ml) sour cream

2 eggs, beaten

1½ cups (170g) strong Cheddar cheese, shredded

1 tsp. granulated sugar substitute

Salt and pepper to taste

DIRECTIONS:

1. Preheat the oven to 375°F (191°C).

2. Prepare a 2 quart casserole

3. Peel and cut up the squash. Place in a food processor and chop finely.

4. Heat the oil in a large skillet and sauté the onion for a minute.

5. Add the squash, season with salt and pepper and cook in the skillet for about 5 minutes.

6. Add the garlic and sauté for an extra minute.

7. Remove the squash mixture from the heat and spoon it into the prepared casserole dish.

8. In a bowl mix together the chili, sour cream, 1 cup cheese and some seasoning.

9. Add the egg and mix well together.

10. Add this chili mixture to the squash and blend well together.

11. Sprinkle with the remaining cheese.

12. Put the dish into the oven and bake for about 25 minutes until the topping turns golden brown.

Nutritional Facts per portion: Calories 175, Fat 13.0g, Carbohydrate 7.6g, Dietary Fiber 1.7g, Net Carbs 5.9g, Protein 8.0g.

SNACKS

GINGER CHICKEN WINGS

An eastern flavor adds a zing to this snack which will become an all-time favourite!

Serves 6

INGREDIENTS:

1¾ pounds (795g) chicken wings

1 cup (237ml) light soy sauce

¼ cup (59ml) white wine

2 cloves garlic, finely chopped

2 tbsp. granulated sugar substitute

¼ cup (59ml) sesame oil

½ tsp. ground ginger

DIRECTIONS:

1. Wash the chicken wings and pat dry on a paper towel.

2. Cut into piece at the joints, discard the wing tips.

3. Spread the chicken out on a shallow baking dish leaving a space between them.

4. In a small bowl combine the rest of the ingredients and mix well.

5. Pour over the wing pieces. Marinade for at least 12 hours or overnight.

6. Pre-heat the oven to 350°F (177°C).

7. Bake the wings for about an hour and a quarter. Serve warm with plenty of serviettes!

Nutritional Facts per portion: Calories 367, Fat 18.9g, Carbohydrate 4.5g, Dietary Fiber 0g, Net Carbs 4.5g, Protein 41.1g.

MINI PIZZAS WITH PESTO

Amazingly easy! Amazingly quick! And a taste magnet that'll bring you back for second helpings, or more! How's that for a recommendation?

Makes 12

INGREDIENTS:

12 ounces (340g) tasty breakfast sausage, skinned

1 egg, whisked

½ tsp. Italian seasoning

¼ cup (59ml) spaghetti sauce

¼ cup (59ml) basil pesto

5 ounces (142g) mozzarella cheese, grated

½ red bell pepper, sliced very thinly

DIRECTIONS:

1. Pre-heat the oven to 350°F (177°C) and prepare 12 muffin cups.

2. In a medium sized bowl mix together the sausage meat, egg and Italian seasoning using your hands.

3. Divide into 12 portions and press each portion in the base of a muffin cup.

4. Bake in the pre-heated oven for 12 – 15 minutes. Drain away any excess fat.

5. Divide the spaghetti sauce among the cups, followed by the pesto and then sprinkle with mozzarella cheese.

6. Put back into the oven for another 10 minutes.

7. Cool and lift carefully out of the cups onto a serving platter. Top with the red bell pepper strips.

Nutritional Facts per portion: Calories 145, Fat 11.0g, Carbohydrate 1.8g, Dietary Fiber 0.3g, Net Carbs 1.5g, Protein 9.2g.

MINI QUICHES

Make a batch of these to eat now or keep in the fridge to pop in a lunch box!

Makes 12

INGREDIENTS:

20 ounces (567g) Colby jack cheese or mild Cheddar, shredded

4 tbsp. butter

1 large onion, finely chopped

12 large eggs, cracked and whisked

2 cups (478g) heavy cream

Salt and pepper to season

3 tsp. dried thyme

12 large paper muffin cups

DIRECTIONS:

1. Pre-heat the oven to 350°F (177°C).

2. Melt 2 tbsp. butter in a skillet over a medium low heat and sauté the onion until soft and translucent.

3. Set aside and cool.

4. Melt the rest of the butter and brush the inside of the muffin cups.

5. Sprinkle half of the shredded cheese over the bottoms of the muffin cups.

6. Add half of the onion, evenly distributed.

7. Add the cream to the whisked eggs along with the seasoning and thyme.

8. Pour evenly into the muffin cups and gently mix in the onion and cheese.

9. Bake in the oven for 10 minutes, turn and continue baking until cooked for another 5 minutes or so.

10. Remove from the oven, cool and serve.

11. Use any other vegetables you may have or even some chopped salami to make a change.

12. Remember to factor any additions into the calorie and carb. count!

Nutritional Facts per portion: Calories 364, Fat 31.3g, Carbohydrate 3.9g, Dietary Fiber 0.9g, Net Carbs 3.0g, Protein 16.9g.

CRISPY CHICKEN DIPPING STRIPS

Keto friendly and so very good – you will be asking for more!

Makes 12 strips

INGREDIENTS:

12 chicken tenderloins

2 tbsp. almond flour

2 tbsp. flax meal

3 tbsp. Parmesan cheese, grated finely

1 large fresh egg

Seasoning salt to taste

Olive oil for frying

DIRECTIONS:

1. Place the flour, flax meal, cheese and seasoning in a bowl and mix well together.

2. In a separate bowl beat the egg.

3. Dip each chicken tenderloin into the egg and then into the flour mix. Coat really well.

4. Pour some olive oil into a skillet to a depth of about ½ inch (1.25cm).

5. Heat over a high heat until very hot.

6. Fry the chicken in the hot oil until cooked and crisp. Turn over half way through cooking – about 6 minutes all together.

7. Remove the chicken from the oil and drain well on paper towel. Serve hot with your favourite dipping sauce.

Nutritional Facts per portion: Calories 107, Fat 6.4g, Carbohydrate 0.7g, Dietary Fiber 0.3g, Net Carbs 0.4g, Protein 12.6g.

SAUTÉED EGGY MUSHROOMS

Veggie or snack! These mushrooms could be both as they are tasty with bacon, a piece of steak or just on their own!

Serves 6

INGREDIENTS:

8 ounces (227g) mushrooms, chopped

4 tbsp. butter

1 clove garlic, minced

2 tsp. parsley, chopped

8 large eggs

2 tbsp. heavy cream

1 ounce (28g) Parmesan cheese, grated

Salt and pepper to season

DIRECTIONS:

1. Melt half of the butter in a skillet and sauté the mushrooms and garlic until tender.

2. Remove from the skillet and set aside.

3. Beat together the eggs and the cream. Add some seasoning and whisk it in.

4. Scramble the eggs in the remaining butter, until creamy.

5. Stir in the mushrooms, garlic and parsley.

6. Sprinkle with Parmesan cheese.

7. Serve hot.

Nutritional Facts per portion: Calories 205, Fat 17.3g, Carbohydrate 2.3g, Dietary Fiber 0g, Net Carbs 2.3g, Protein 11.3g.

CHEESY ZUCCHINI ROLLS WITH OLIVES

These tasty sides have goat cheese in them but you could easily substitute cream cheese if you preferred!

Makes 18 rolls

INGREDIENTS:

6 small zucchini, thinly sliced lengthwise – 18 strips

Olive oil

Salt and pepper

3 tbsp. cilantro, chopped

7 ounces (198g) herby goat cheese

12 kalamata olives, finely chopped

DIRECTIONS:

1. Pre-heat a broiler to maximum temperature.

2. Brush the zucchini strips with olive oil and broil until lightly charred and cooked.

3. Remove from heat and season with salt and pepper. Cool.

4. In a small bowl beat the cheese and stir in the chopped olives and cilantro.

5. Divide the cheese mixture evenly among the cooked zucchini strips.

6. Spread it gently along each strip and roll each one up like a Swiss roll.

7. Secure with a toothpick if necessary and serve.

Nutritional Facts per portion: Calories 44, Fat 3.2g, Carbohydrate 1.6g, Dietary Fiber 0.5g, Net Carbs 1.1g, Protein 2.5g.

BACON STUFFED EGGS

Everyone loves stuffed eggs and these will be no different! Bacon and mustard give these treats a smoky zing!

Makes 24 halves

INGREDIENTS:

12 large fresh eggs, hard boiled and peeled

8 strips bacon

3 tbsp. mayonnaise

2 tsp. Dijon mustard

Pinch cayenne pepper

DIRECTIONS:

1. Cut the eggs in half lengthways.

2. Scoop out the yolks with a teaspoon and place them in a bowl.

3. Add the mayonnaise and mustard to the yolks and mix very well together making sure that there are no lumps.

4. Cook the bacon strips until crispy and when cool cut into small pieces.

5. Add half of the bacon to the egg yolk mixture and set the rest aside.

6. Mix the yolk and bacon and using a teaspoon carefully spoon this mixture into the egg white shells leaving it as a pile – do not smooth it down.

7. Sprinkle the eggs with a little cayenne and top with the remaining bacon.

8. Put on a platter and serve.

Nutritional Facts per half: Calories 77, Fat 5.8g, Carbohydrate 0.8g, Dietary Fiber 0g, Net Carbs 0.8g, Protein 5.5g.

CHEESY CHEDDAR CRISPS

Savoury Cheddar cheese biscuits made spicy with a dash of cayenne pepper!

Makes 20 crisps

INGREDIENTS:

2 cups (226g) Cheddar cheese, finely shredded

Chili sauce

DIRECTIONS:

1. Pre-heat the oven to 350°F (177°C).

2. Line 2 baking sheets with non-stick parchment paper.

3. In a medium sized bowl mix together the Cheddar cheese and the chili sauce.

4. Place tablespoonful's in the baking sheets, well apart. Press down lightly with the back of a fork.

5. Place in the oven to cook for about 5 minutes until the crisps are a light golden brown. They brown quickly so be careful!

6. Remove from the oven and let cool for a second or two before removing to a cooling rack.

7. When hot these can be draped over a rolling pin to form taco shapes or formed into tiny cups.

Nutritional Facts per portion: Calories 46, Fat 3.8g, Carbohydrate 0.2g, Dietary Fiber 0g, Net Carbs 0.2g, Protein 2.8g.

CHILI CHICKEN BITES

These are very popular as a cocktail snack or before barbeque snack. Make a double or even a triple quantity to ensure you have enough to share!

Serves 12

INGREDIENTS:

20 ounces (567g) boneless, skinless chicken breast

1 tbsp. olive oil

2 tsp. hot chili sauce

Salt and pepper to taste

16 ounces (454g) back bacon strips

DIRECTIONS:

1. Cut the chicken up into bite sized pieces.

2. Toss in the oil and chili sauce in a medium sized bowl.

3. Cover and place in the fridge to marinate for 1½ hours.

4. Pre-heat the oven to 400°F (204°C).

5. Line a baking pan with foil.

6. Remove the chicken from the fridge and season.

7. Cut each bacon strip into 3 pieces and wrap a piece around each piece of chicken. Secure with a toothpick.

8. Bake in the hot oven for 20 – 25 minutes until the chicken is cooked and the bacon is crisp.

9. Remove from the oven and sprinkle on a little more chili sauce if liked.

Nutritional Facts per portion: Calories 294, Fat 11.0g, Carbohydrate 1.3g, Dietary Fiber 0g, Net Carbs 1.3g, Protein 46.0g.

EGGPLANT MINI PIZZAS

Keto friendly mini pizzas that give a boost to your vegetable intake without too many carbs!

Serves 6

INGREDIENTS:

2 smallish eggplants, peeled and each cut into 6 x half inch (1.25cm) slices

5 tbsp. olive oil

1 tsp. salt

¼ tsp. black pepper

½ cup (119ml) tasty pasta sauce

1 cup (113g) mozzarella cheese, shredded

DIRECTIONS:

1. Pre-heat the oven to 425°F (218°C).

2. Prepare 2 baking trays with non-stick parchment on top.

3. Brush both sides of the eggplant slices with olive oil and place on the prepared baking trays.

4. Season with salt and pepper and bake for 10 minutes until almost cooked.

5. Place 1 tablespoon pasta sauce on each slice and top with shredded cheese.

6. Return to the oven and bake for another 5 – 6 minutes until the cheese is melted.

7. Serve hot.

Nutritional Facts per portion: Calories 218, Fat 16.6g, Carbohydrate 13.9, Dietary Fiber 6.4g, Net Carbs 7.5g, Protein 7.0g.

MUSHROOM CRISPS

A bowl full of these at any time of the day will satisfy even the most discerning. If you would like a spicier crisp, sprinkle on some chili powder or garlic spice!

Serves 4

INGREDIENTS:

12 ounces (340g) large Portobello mushrooms

5 tbsp. butter, melted

¾ tsp. salt

Pinch black pepper

DIRECTIONS:

1. Pre-heat the oven to 300°F (149°C).

2. Line a 2 baking trays with parchment paper

3. Slice the mushrooms thinly and place in a single layer on the baking sheets.

4. Brush the mushroom slices with melted butter.

5. Sprinkle with salt and pepper

6. Place the mushrooms in the oven and bake for 40 – 50 minutes until crisp and golden brown.

7. Rotate the baking trays while the mushrooms are cooking.

8. Remove from the oven and cool.

Nutritional Facts per portion: Calories 146, Fat 14.6g, Carbohydrate 2.8g, Dietary Fiber 0.9g, Net Carbs 1.9g, Protein 2.8g.

MUSHROOMS WITH A CHORIZO STUFFING

Quick and easy to make, these stuffed mushrooms are perfect to make for unexpected guests!

Serves 4

INGREDIENTS:

12 large Portobello mushroom caps

4 ounces (113g) sheep's milk cheese

6 ounces (170g) chorizo sausage, skinless

1 egg

1 small onion, finely diced

1 tsp. parsley, chopped

Black pepper

Coconut oil for greasing

DIRECTIONS:

1. Pre-heat the oven to 350°F (177°C).

2. Grease a baking tray with coconut oil.

3. Mix together all of the ingredients except the mushroom caps.

4. Spoon this mixture into the mushroom caps and place on the baking tray.

5. Place the tray in the oven and bake for about 20 minutes until brown and cooked.

6. Remove from the oven and cool for a few minutes.

7. Serve 3 mushroom caps to each person.

Nutritional Facts per portion: Calories 281, Fat 23.6g, Carbohydrate 2.3g, Dietary Fiber 0.6g, Net Carbs 1.9g, Protein 16.2g.

PIZZA WITH CAULIFLOWER CRUST

A wonderful alternative recipe for Saturday night pizza at home!

Serves 4

INGREDIENTS:

2 cups (248g) cauliflower, grated

½ cup (50g) Parmesan cheese, grated

1 garlic clove, finely chopped

¼ tsp. sea salt

½ tbsp. fresh basil, chopped

1 large fresh egg

2 tbsp. coconut flour

1 tbsp. olive oil

½ tsp. garlic salt

½ cup (119ml) marinara sauce

¼ cup (56g) chorizo sausage

2 ounces (57g) bacon

2 tbsp. button mushrooms, chopped

¼ cup (31g) red bell peppers, chopped

Extra Parmesan for sprinkling

DIRECTIONS:

1. Pre-heat the oven to 450°F (232°C).

2. Cover 2 baking trays with parchment paper.

3. Steam the grated cauliflower until al dente.

4. Cool and then combine with the Parmesan, garlic, salt, basil, and egg and coconut flour.

5. Mix well to form a soft dough.

6. Divide the mixture into 2 and form an 8 inch (20cm) round on each of the two prepared baking trays.

7. Use a spoon and your hands to make them as round as possible.

8. Sprinkle with the garlic salt and bake in the hot oven for 12 – 15 minutes until browned at the edges.

9. Sauté the sausage, bacon, onion, mushrooms and pepper over a medium high heat until cooked through and the vegetables are soft.

10. Remove the pizza crust from the oven and let it cool for a while.

11. Divide the topping between the two crusts and sprinkle with extra Parmesan cheese.

12. Return to the oven and turn on the broiler.

13. Broil for about 5 minutes until the cheese has melted.

14. Slice and serve.

Nutritional Facts per portion: Calories 309, Fat 22.3g, Carbohydrate 10.4g, Dietary Fiber 3.5g, Net Carbs 6.9g, Protein 16.5g.

CHEESE SNACK BALL

Make this as the centrepiece for a buffet table. Your guests can have it with crackers, you with crispy celery or cucumber strips.

Serves 24

INGREDIENTS:

16 ounces (454g) full fat cream cheese

1½ cups (170g) Cheddar cheese, shredded

2 slices of bacon, crisped and crumbled

1 tbsp. dried parsley

4 tsp. fresh chives, chopped

1 tsp. garlic powder

¼ tsp. dried dill

½ tsp. black pepper

½ cup (69g) sliced almonds, toasted

1 red bell pepper, roasted and sliced

DIRECTIONS:

1. Mix together all of the herbs and spices in a large bowl.

2. Mix in the cream cheese.

3. Add the bacon and Cheddar cheese.

4. Shape into 2 'balls', flatten slightly and roll in the toasted almonds.

5. Place on a serving plate and decorate with the pepper strips.

6. Refrigerate until needed.

Nutritional Facts per portion: Calories 119, Fat 11.0g, Carbohydrate 1.5g, Dietary Fiber 0.6g, Net Carbs 0.9g, Protein 4.0g.

SWEET ENDINGS

VANILLA PUDDING

Mmmmm... A delightful Keto vanilla pudding. Who said Keto can't be a snack filled heaven?

Serves 4

INGREDIENTS:

1 cup (239g) heavy cream

1 cup (237ml) water

¼ tsp. salt

½ cup (100g) granulated sugar substitute

2 tsp. xanthan gum

2 egg yolks

2 tsp. butter

1 tsp. vanilla

DIRECTIONS:

1. In a small sauce pan whisk together the cream, salt, water and sweetener.

2. Sprinkle the gum over the surface and whisk in.

3. Whisk in the egg yolks.

4. Heat over a low heat stirring continuously until thick.

5. Whisk in the butter and vanilla.

6. Divide among 4 small desert dishes.

7. Chill before serving.

Nutritional Facts per portion: Calories 156, Fat 15.3g, Carbohydrate 3.3g, Dietary Fiber 0.8g, Net Carbs 2.5g, Protein 2.1g.

CHOCOLATE VANILLA BROWNIES

These brownies have chia seeds in them to add a healthy dose of Omega-3 to your diet. Serve with Keto friendly ice cream or a dollop of whipped heavy cream for a dessert worthy of second helpings.

Serves 12

INGREDIENTS:

1 tbsp. chia seeds

½ cup (119ml) water

4 ounces (113ml) butter, melted

¼ cup (28g) coconut flour

¼ cup (28g) flax seed meal

1½ cups (300g) granulated sugar substitute

¾ cup (65g) unsweetened cocoa powder

4 large fresh eggs, beaten

2 tsp. vanilla extract

½ tsp. baking soda

½ tsp. salt

4 ounces (113g) cream cheese

DIRECTIONS:

1. Pre-heat the oven to 325°F (163°C).

2. Grease an 8 x 8 inch (20 x 20cm) baking pan.

3. Mix the chia seeds with the water and set aside for 20 minutes to form a gel. Stir half way through this time.

4. In a large bowl mix together the chia gel, flour and flax meal.

5. Whisk in the eggs.

6. Add in the rest of the ingredients. Mix lightly, do not beat.

7. Pour the batter into the prepared baking pan.

8. Warm the cream cheese.

9. Place small spoonful's of cream cheese onto the batter and with the back of a knife swirl the cheese into the chocolate mixture.

10. Place in the oven and bake for about 45 minutes until a toothpick inserted into the center comes out clean.

11. Remove from the oven and cool.

12. Leave in a cool place for 24 hours before slicing into 12 pieces.

Nutritional Facts per portion: Calories 182, Fat 15.4g, Carbohydrate 6.8g, Dietary Fiber 4.7g, Net Carbs 2.1g, Protein 5.7g.

CHOCOLATE ICE CREAM

A smooth chocolate ice-cream with a hint of almond and vanilla!

Serves 12

INGREDIENTS:

4 cups (956g) heavy cream

1 cup (237ml) unsweetened almond milk

8 egg yolks

½ cup (100g) powdered sugar substitute

1 tsp. vanilla essence

8 ounces (227g) dark chocolate, 75% cocoa solids, melted and cooled

---

DIRECTIONS:

1. Mix all of the ingredients together and place in an ice-cream machine.

2. Churn until solid.

3. Place in the freezer.

4. If you do not have an ice-cream machine – no matter.

5. Mix the ingredients as before and pour into a freezer proof container.

6. Place in the freezer and mix with a fork every hour or so to break up the crystals that may form.

7. Freeze until hard.

8. Remove the ice cream from the freezer about 10 minutes before serving to allow it to soften slightly.

Nutritional Facts per portion: Calories 293, Fat 23.6g, Carbohydrate 7.8g, Dietary Fiber 2.4g, Net Carbs 5.4g, Protein 4.6g.

COFFEE ICE CREAM

Low carb and sporting a superb flavor! Homemade is definitely best!

Serves 12

INGREDIENTS:

4 cups (956g) heavy cream

1 cup (237ml) unsweetened almond milk

8 egg yolks

½ cup (50g) strong coffee beans

½ cup (100g) granulated sugar substitute

1 tsp. vanilla extract

½ tsp. xanthan gum

¼ tsp. salt

DIRECTIONS:

1. In a medium bowl stir together the coffee beans, cream and almond milk.

2. Leave for the coffee flavor to infuse for at least 3 hours, longer for a stronger flavor.

3. Heat the cream mixture gently in a sauce pan over a low heat.

4. Bring to a simmering point. Strain out the coffee beans.

5. Return the cream to the pan and add the egg yolks, sugar substitute, vanilla, salt and xanthan gum.

6. Stir well and place over a low heat.

7. Stirring continuously warm the mixture to a simmer and cook until a thick custard is formed.

8. Remove from the heat and pass through a sieve to strain any lumps that may have formed.

9. Chill until completely cold.

10. Place in an ice cream machine and churn until frozen.

11. Or freeze in a freezer proof dish placed in the freezer, stirring frequently to break up any ice crystals that may form.

12. Remove from the freezer 10 minutes before serving to soften a little.

Nutritional Facts per portion: Calories 180, Fat 18.0g, Carbohydrate 2.2g, Dietary Fiber 0g, Net Carbs 2.2g, Protein 2.7g.

MINTY CHOCOLATE CHIP ICE

You will think you have visited Utopia when you taste this ambrosial dessert! Wow!

Serves 8

INGREDIENTS:

2 cups (478g) heavy cream

1 cup (239g) light cream

1 tsp. liquid stevia extract (adjust to taste)

4 – 5 drops peppermint extract (to taste)

4 – 5 drops green food coloring

2 ounces (57g) dark chocolate, chopped

DIRECTIONS:

1. In a medium bowl whisk together all of the ingredients except the chocolate.

2. Pour it into an ice cream machine and churn until nearly done.

3. Add the chopped chocolate.

4. Serve or store covered in the freezer.

5. If you don't have an ice cream machine place the mixture into a freezer container and freeze until solid, stirring ever half an hour until thick and ice crystal free.

Nutritional Facts per portion: Calories 185, Fat 17.8g, Carbohydrate 5.5g, Dietary Fiber 0g, Net Carbs 5.5g, Protein 1.5g.

LEMONY CHEESECAKE

A creamy baked dessert with a hint of lemon!

Serves 16

INGREDIENTS:

6 ounces (170g) almond flour

2 ounces (57g) butter, chilled

½ cup (100g) granulated sugar substitute

½ tsp. xanthan gum

¼ tsp. salt

8 drops liquid stevia extract (adjust to taste)

12 ounces (340g) cream cheese, softened

1 large egg

2 tbsp. heavy cream

1 lemon, zested

2 tbsp. lemon juice

DIRECTIONS:

1. Pre-heat the oven to 350°F (177°C).

2. Line an 8 x 8 inch (20 x 20cm) cake pan with parchment.

3. Combine the first six ingredients in a food processor until the mixture resembles bread crumbs.

4. Press into the prepared cake pan in an even layer.

5. Bake in the oven for 12 minutes. Set aside and cool.

6. Reduce the oven heat to 275°F (135°C).

7. Beat the cream cheese until smooth and add the rest of the ingredients.

8. Spread this mixture over the cooled crust and bake for 25 – 30 minutes.

9. The filling should be barely set – do not overcook!

10. Remove from the oven and cool.

11. Place in the fridge and chill for at least 2½ hours.

12. Cut into slices and serve.

Nutritional Facts per portion: Calories 173, Fat 16.6g, Carbohydrate 3.5g, Dietary Fiber 1.3g, Net Carbs 2.2g, Protein 4.4g.

KETO TIRAMISU

This pudding has a wonderful flavor and could easily be mistaken for the 'real' thing!

Serves 4

INGREDIENTS:

8 eggs

1 cup (96g) almond flour

8 tbsp. powdered sugar substitute

½ tsp. baking powder

10 ounces (284g) mascarpone cheese

¼ cup (60g) heavy cream

1 tsp. vanilla extract

1 cup (237ml) strong black coffee, sweetened with sugar substitute

Cocoa powder to decorate

DIRECTIONS:

1. Pre-heat the oven into 400°F (204°C).

2. Using parchment paper, line a 6 inch (15cm) round cake tin.

3. Separate 4 of the eggs and beat the yolks with 3 tablespoons of the sugar powder.

4. Fold in the almond flour and baking powder.

5. Beat the egg whites until stiff peaks form.

6. Fold the egg whites into the cake batter.

7. Spoon into the prepared cake tin.

8. Place in the oven and bake for 10 minutes until cooked.

9. Remove and cool on a cake rack.

10. Separate the other 4 eggs and place the yolks into a small heat proof bowl.

11. Add 2½ tablespoons sugar powder and whisk until blended.

12. Place the bowl on top of a small saucepan of simmering water and stir constantly until it forms thick custard.

13. Pour the custard into a clean cool bowl and beat in the mascarpone and vanilla together with the rest of the sugar powder.

14. Beat the egg whites and cream together until stiff peaks are formed.

15. Carefully fold this into the cooled custard.

16. In a glass bowl, place the sponge on the base.

17. Pour over the sweetened coffee.

18. Add the custard and distribute it evenly over the top.

19. Dust with the cocoa powder.

20. Refrigerate for at least 2 hours, or even better overnight.

Nutritional Facts per portion: Calories 333, Fat 24.9g, Carbohydrate 6.8g, Dietary Fiber 0.9g, Net Carbs 5.9g, Protein 21.1g.

REFRIGERATOR CHEESECAKE

A special cheesecake which you can top with different sugar free products as you wish! Sugar free cherry jam is a must!

Serves 8

INGREDIENTS:

1½ cups (144g) almond meal

3 tbsp. butter, melted

¾ cup (150g) powdered sugar substitute

10 ounces (284g) cream cheese

2 tsp. vanilla extract

1 tsp. lemon juice

1 cup (239g) heavy cream

DIRECTIONS:

1. Pre-heat the oven to 350°F (177°C).

2. Line a 9 inch (23cm) pie pan with parchment paper.

3. Melt the butter and add to the almond meal with ¼ cup of powdered sugar substitute.

4. Mix well and press into the bottom of the pie pan.

5. Bake in the pre-heated oven for 10 minutes. Be careful it does not get too brown. Remove from the oven and cool.

6. Mix the cream cheese, the rest of the sweetener, the vanilla and the lemon juice together in a medium sized bowl.

7. In a separate bowl whisk the cream until it peaks.

8. Mix the cream gently into the cheese mixture.

9. Spread over the baked base in an even layer.

10. Refrigerate for a few hours before serving.

Nutritional Facts per portion: Calories 341, Fat 32.8g, Carbohydrate 7.0g, Dietary Fiber 2.2g, Net Carbs 4.8g, Protein 7.5g.

STRAWBERRY ICED CHEESECAKE

Spoil yourself with some fresh strawberries atop this vanilla cheesecake!

Serves 6

INGREDIENTS:

1 cup (96g) almond meal

2 tbsp. butter, melted

2 tsp. vanilla extract

½ tsp. liquid stevia extract (adjust to taste)

Pinch salt

6 ounces (170g) fresh strawberries, hulled

12 ounces (340g) cream cheese

¾ cup (178ml) sour cream

1 cup (200g) granulated sugar substitute

DIRECTIONS:

1. Pre-heat the oven to 350°F (177°C).

2. Grease a 9 inch (23cm) pie plate with a little butter.

3. Mix together the almond meal, butter, stevia, half the vanilla and the salt until it forms crumbs.

4. Put into the base of the pie plate and place in the hot oven.

5. Bake for 10 minutes. Stir half way through the cooking time to brown the crumbs on all sides.

6. Remove from the oven and cool.

7. Divide the crumbs equally among 6 individual serving dishes.

8. Press down a little so they come a bit up the side of each dish.

9. Place the strawberries in a food processor along with the rest of the ingredients.

10. Pulse until smooth.

11. Spoon into the serving dishes on top of the crumbs.

12. Chill well before serving.

13. Top with an extra strawberry and some heavy cream if liked — just remember to add any carbs!

Nutritional Facts per portion: Calories 420, Fat 39.1g, Carbohydrate 10.5g, Dietary Fiber 2.6g, Net Carbs 7.9g, Protein 9.4g.

CHOCOLATE JELLY

The chocolate, coconut flavor of this dessert is quite refreshing and makes a great ending to a dinner or lunch!

Serves 4

INGREDIENTS:

2 cups (474ml) full fat coconut milk

4 tbsp. cocoa powder

¾ tsp. liquid stevia extract (adjust to taste)

2 tbsp. sugar free gelatine

4 tbsp. water

DIRECTIONS:

1. Place a sauce pan over a medium heat and add the coconut milk, cocoa and stevia to it.

2. Soak the gelatine in the cold water.

3. Add the gelatine to the milk mixture and stir until dissolved.

4. When the mixture is warm and everything is combined, pour into 4 small ramekin dishes.

5. Place in the fridge for an hour to set.

6. Serve with extra cream, whipped and piped on top if you fancy.

Nutritional Facts per portion: Calories 288, Fat 29.3g, Carbohydrate 9.6g, Dietary Fiber 4.2g, Net Carbs 5.4g, Protein 3.8g.

DARK CHOCOLATE MOUSSE

Serve with whipped heavy cream or whipped coconut cream to mark a special occasion! This is a bit higher in carbs but try to factor it in for a treat!

Serves 8

INGREDIENTS:

4 ounces (113g) dark chocolate, 75% cocoa butter

6 tbsp. water

Pinch salt

½ cup (118ml) coconut cream, chilled

½ tsp. almond extract

DIRECTIONS:

1. Place the water, salt and chocolate into a small pan and heat over a low heat until the chocolate is melted.

2. Place in a medium sized bowl and beat with an electric hand mixer until a fluffy mousse-like consistency is reached. This may take up to 5 minutes.

3. Spoon the mouse into individual glass serving dishes and refrigerate until needed.

4. When nearly ready to serve, beat the coconut cream with the almond extract with the electric hand mixer until thick and it holds its shape. Again about 5 minutes.

5. Place a dollop on each chocolate mousse and serve.

Nutritional Facts per portion: Calories 120, Fat 8.7g, Carbohydrate 9.5g, Dietary Fiber 0.9g, Net Carbs 8.6g, Protein 1.5g.

NUTTY CHEESCAKE NIBBLES

Serve after dinner or as a dessert type snack at a cocktail party. These nibbles are popular with children and it might be a great idea to make a double quantity.

Makes 16

INGREDIENTS:

8 ounce (227g) packet of full fat cream cheese

¼ cup (21g) unsweetened powdered cocoa

Liquid stevia extract (adjust number of drops to taste)

1 tbsp. sugar free hazel nut syrup

¼ cup (18g) ground hazelnuts

DIRECTIONS:

1. Soften the cream cheese and beat until extra creamy – an electric mixer will help with this.

2. Add all of the other ingredients except the chopped nuts.

3. Mix well together.

4. Roll the mixture into 16 balls, damp hands will help!

5. Roll each ball into the ground nuts.

6. Place in small mini muffin paper cases.

7. Keep in the fridge until ready to serve.

Nutritional Facts per portion: Calories 60, Fat 5.8g, Carbohydrate 1.4g, Dietary Fiber 0.6g, Net Carbs 0.8g, Protein 1.5g.

COCONUT CHOCOLATE BALLS

Easy to prepare treats for "need a treat" moments!

Makes 24

INGREDIENTS:

1 cup (239g) heavy cream

3½ ounces (99g) dark chocolate, 75% cocoa solids

2 ounces (57g) butter

1 tsp. vanilla extract

3 cups (288g) almond flour

Coconut flakes

DIRECTIONS:

1. Break the chocolate into small pieces.

2. Put the cream in a small sauce pan over a low heat.

3. Add the chocolate to the cream and heat the two together until the chocolate has melted.

4. Add the butter and stir until the mixture thickens.

5. Stir in the vanilla and the almond flour.

6. Roll the mixture into 24 balls and dip them into coconut flakes.

7. Put the balls on a plate and refrigerate until hard.

8. Serve and enjoy!

Nutritional Facts per portion: Calories 139, Fat 12.7g, Carbohydrate 5.2g, Dietary Fiber 1.6g, Net Carbs 3.6g, Protein 3.6g.

CREAMY COCONUT CANDY

This coconut creamy treat with dark chocolate chips is an exquisite snack.

Makes 24

INGREDIENTS:

2 cups (474ml) concentrated coconut cream

1½ (356ml) cups coconut oil

¼ tsp. liquid stevia extract (adjust to taste)

1 cup (237ml) macadamia nut butter

1 cup (115g) macadamia nuts, chopped

1 cup (170g) dark chocolate chips

2 tsp. vanilla essence

DIRECTIONS:

1. Warm the coconut cream to allow it to be easily stirred.

2. In a large bowl mix the coconut cream with all of the other ingredients except the nuts and the chocolate chips.

3. Use an electric mixer to make this a little easier.

4. Prepare two cookie sheets by lining them with parchment paper.

5. Spread out the nuts and chocolate chips on the parchment.

6. Pour over the coconut cream mixture.

7. Place in the freezer to set.

8. Break into 24 even sized pieces and serve immediately.

9. Store in the freezer if there is any left!

Nutritional Facts per portion: Calories 341, Fat 35.9g, Carbohydrate 6.8g, Dietary Fiber 3.1g, Net Carbs 3.7g, Protein 2.7g.

PEANUT BUTTER COOKIES

Traditional flavors are always popular as lunch boxes treats too!

Makes 32

INGREDIENTS:

½ cup (119ml) smooth peanut butter

¼ cup (59ml) farm butter

2 large eggs

⅔ cup (156ml) coconut oil

½ tsp. vanilla extract

½ tsp. baking soda

¼ tsp. salt

½ cup (56g) coconut flour

DIRECTIONS:

1. Pre-heat the oven into 350°F (177°C).

2. Using baking parchment paper, line 2 cookie trays

3. Cream together the peanut butter, butter, eggs, coconut oil and vanilla in a medium sized bowl.

4. Stir in the flour, baking soda and the salt.

5. Make 32 small balls of mixture and place them on the cookie trays.

6. Flatten them slightly with a fork.

7. Place in the oven and bake for 10 – 12 minutes until brown.

8. Cool on the tray for a few minutes before moving to a wire rack.

Nutritional Facts per portion: Calories 88, Fat 8.5g, Carbohydrate 1.8g, Dietary Fiber 0.9g, Net Carbs 0.9g, Protein 1.6g.

COCONUT CHEWS

Guess you are going to be caught dipping into these treats. Enjoy!

Makes 45

INGREDIENTS:

1½ ounces (43g) almond flour

¼ tsp. baking powder

Pinch salt

2 large eggs

1 tsp. vanilla extract

¼ tsp. almond extract

¾ cup (150g) granulated sugar substitute

1 tbsp. butter, melted

8 ounces (227g) unsweetened coconut

DIRECTIONS:

1. Pre-heat the oven into 325°F (163°C).

2. Using baking parchment paper, line 2 large cookie trays.

3. Mix together the flour, baking powder and salt in a bowl.

4. In a separate bowl mix together the eggs and extracts and beat well.

5. Beat the sugar substitute into the eggs. Blend in the melted butter.

6. Add the dry ingredients and then the coconut. Mix well.

7. Drop tablespoonfuls onto the parchment paper lined trays.

8. Bake in the oven for 12 – 15 minutes until brown around the edges.

9. Be careful the chews do not burn.

10. Cool on a wire rack and serve.

Nutritional Facts per portion: Calories 29, Fat 2.6g, Carbohydrate 1.1g, Dietary Fiber 0.6g, Net Carbs 0.5g, Protein 0.7g.

PANCAKES KETO STYLE

A useful recipe to have up your sleeve for a dessert or afternoon tea!

Makes 6

INGREDIENTS:

4 ounces (113g) cream cheese

4 eggs

6 drops liquid stevia extract (adjust to taste)

1 tsp. cinnamon powder

Butter for cooking

DIRECTIONS:

1. Place all of the ingredients in a blender and blend until smooth.

2. Leave to rest for 5 minutes to settle and become bubble free.

3. Heat a small crepe pan and grease it lightly with butter.

4. Pour in enough mixture to cover the bottom of the pan thinly.

5. Cook until golden.

6. Flip and cook the other side.

7. Repeat with the rest of the batter.

8. Serve with some sugar free syrup of your choice or fresh berries and cream.

Nutritional Facts per portion: Calories 133, Fat 12.2g, Carbohydrate 1.0g, Dietary Fiber 0g, Net Carbs 1.0g, Protein 5.2g.

ALMOND AND GOJI MUFFINS

Nutritious and delicious, these scrumptious muffins will have you coming back for more!

Makes 10

INGREDIENTS:

1 ounce (28g) butter, melted

4 fresh farm eggs

4 tbsp. grape seed oil

1 tbsp. almond oil

3 tbsp. almond flour

1 tbsp. flaxseed flour

¼ cup (60g) light cream

1 tsp. liquid stevia extract (adjust to taste)

1 tsp. baking powder

Pinch of salt

2 tbsp. dried goji berries, ground

DIRECTIONS:

1. Pre-heat the oven to 350°F (177°C).

2. Prepare 10 muffin cups and place on a baking tray.

3. Break the eggs into a medium sized bowl and beat well together.

4. Add the oils and continue beating until thick and creamy.

5. Add the cream, a little at a time beating well between each addition.

6. Beat the melted butter into the mixture and then the liquid sweetener.

7. In a separate bowl mix together all of the other ingredients.

8. Add these to the egg mixture, one spoon at a time and mix gently so that you do not knock all of the air out of the egg mixture.

9. Spoon into the muffin cases and bake for 15 minutes.

10. The muffins will have risen and be golden.

11. Serve warm.

Nutritional Facts per portion: Calories 137, Fat 13.4g, Carbohydrate 2.1g, Dietary Fiber 0.5g, Net Carbs 1.6g, Protein 2.9g.

CHOCOLATE CUPCAKES

Keto-friendly treats with a mocha flavor!

Makes 12

INGREDIENTS:

2 farm fresh eggs, separated

4 scoops low carb chocolate protein powder

10 ounces (284g) mascarpone

½ ounce (14g) unsweetened cocoa powder

¼ cup (237ml) strong coffee, unsweetened and cooled

½ ounce (14g) flax seed, ground

¾ tsp. liquid stevia extract (adjust to taste)

½ tsp. vanilla essence

DIRECTIONS:

1. Pre-heat the oven into 325°F (163°C).

2. Prepare 10 cupcake cases and place on a baking tray.

3. Beat the egg whites until stiff in a large bowl.

4. Mix half of the protein powder with the cocoa and flax seed.

5. Fold into the beaten egg white.

6. In a separate bowl beat half of the mascarpone and fold it into the egg mixture.

7. Pour into the prepared cases and bake for 15 – 18 minutes.

8. Remove from the oven and cool.

9. While the cakes are cooling, make the icing by beating together the egg yolks, remaining protein powder, remaining mascarpone, vanilla and ½ teaspoon of stevia.

10. Mix the other half of the stevia into the coffee and carefully spoon it over each cupcake.

11. Leave to soak in for a while before topping with the icing.

12. Chill before serving.

Nutritional Facts per portion: Calories 79, Fat 4.6g, Carbohydrate 2.1g, Dietary Fiber 1.0g, Net Carbs 1.1g, Protein 7.5g.

SNICKERDOODLES

Cinnamon treats for tea, anyone?

Makes 16

INGREDIENTS:

4 ounces (113g) butter

1 cup (96g) almond flour, generous

1 cup (200g) granulated sugar substitute

1 farm fresh egg

½ tsp. vanilla extract

½ tsp. baking powder

2 tbsp. granulated sugar substitute (for sprinkling)

1 tsp. powdered cinnamon

DIRECTIONS:

1. Prepare two baking sheets by lining with silicone paper.

2. Place all of the ingredients except the sugar topping and cinnamon in a mixing bowl and mix well together.

3. Cover and place in the fridge for about an hour until it has chilled.

4. Divide the mixture into 16 portions and roll each into a ball with your hands. Refrigerate again if the mixture become sticky.

5. Mix the 2 tablespoons sugar substitute with the cinnamon and roll the balls in this mixture.

6. Place the balls on the baking sheets and place in the fridge again for 10 minutes to firm.

Nutritional Facts per portion: Calories 97, Fat 9.5g, Carbohydrate 2.2g, Dietary Fiber 0.8g, Net Carbs 1.4g, Protein 1.9g.

THANK YOU

If you enjoyed these recipes, and I'm guessing your taste buds did, please look for other titles in the Keto Living range.

If you fancy some delicious treats, you may enjoy;

Keto Living 2: Lose Weight with 101 Yummy & Low Carb Ketogenic Savory and Sweet Snacks

For another all course recipe book, replete with beautiful photography look for;

Keto Living 3 - Color Cookbook: Lose Weight with 101 All New Delicious & Low Carb Ketogenic Recipes,

And now available, a guide to the unique protocol of Fat Fasting;

Keto Living – Fat Fast Cookbook: A Guide to Fasting for Weight Loss Including 50 Low Carb & High Fat Recipes

Thanks so much to my family, my friends and the Keto community for keeping me loving all things Keto and making me smile every day.

Be good to each other!

Ella Coleman

35176413R00101

Made in the USA
Lexington, KY
01 September 2014